Quiet Times with Active Preschoolers

Activity Devotions for Families with Young Children

Denise J. Williamson

Augsburg ■ Minneapolis

249
wil

For Joel and Joshua

QUIET TIMES WITH ACTIVE PRESCHOOLERS
Activity Devotions for Families with Young Children

Cover design: Lecy Design

Library of Congress Cataloging-in-Publication Data

Williamson, Denise J., 1954–
   Quiet times with active preschoolers : activity devotions for
families with young children / Denise J. Williamson.
     p.   cm.
   Bibliography: p.
   ISBN 0-8066-2417-5
   1. Family—Prayer-books and devotions—English. 2. Preschool
children—Prayer-books and devotions—English. I. Title.
BV255.W485 1989
249—dc20
                                      89-35831
                                          CIP

The paper used in this publication meets the minimum requirements of American National Standard for Information Sciences—Permanence of Paper for Printed Library Materials, ANSI Z329.48-1984. (∞)™

Manufactured in the U.S.A.   AF 9-2417

93   92   91   90   89   1   2   3   4   5   6   7   9   10

0Sep92 - gift

Contents

Preface

If you have a preschooler in your home, you don't have time for lengthy book introductions. Even now your little one might be eyeing the jam for a tea party with Teddy Bear. I know. I have two active preschoolers of my own.

This book is about having quiet times with active preschoolers like yours and mine. I'm not talking about the "sit-up-at-the-table-nicely-while-company's-here" kind of quiet times. I'm talking about those precious, quality moments when a little child senses the possibility of being friends with God.

Jesus said, "For where two or three come together in my name, there am I with them" (Matt. 18:20). My husband and I want our children to know the truth of Jesus' words. We first tried having family devotions when our older son was two and our younger son was just an infant. Our initial attempt didn't last a week. Out of frustration because of our two tots' restlessness, we began experimenting with activity-oriented quiet times tailored to our children's interests and skills. This book is a gathering of ideas from the months of quiet times we have had with our children since making that change.

Though every family juggles a different assortment of demands and interests, I believe that any Christian parent can have devotions with his or her preschooler. In fact, I'm convinced that parents miss a blessed, God-given opportunity when they don't. Preschoolers thrive on parental attention. They copy parental behavior and emulate their parent's beliefs. These traits probably make it easier to establish regular quiet times with preschoolers than with children of any other age. Yet, too often, adults miss the joys of bringing young children before the throne of God because they believe preschoolers are too young for devotions.

Whether your child is a babe in arms or a youngster crossing off the days until the school bus comes, you can start today to have your own regular family quiet time. What a joy to know that playrooms and backyards are places worthy of encounters with God. Even if your child is dreaming up a party with Teddy Bear right now, you can go knowing that Jesus, too, will be there. It is just this sort of daily experience that sets the stage for *Quiet Times with Active Preschoolers.*

1

Preparing Your Own Heart

Devotions for Parents

A child's experience of God is real. It is as real as the love in his life.
—Anna B. Mow, *Preparing Your Child to Love God*

Since a preschooler mixes secular and sacred thoughts all day long, a quiet time can come as the parent capitalizes on the child's momentary thoughts of God. Think of the things preschoolers say. While putting together a puzzle of the United States, my four-year-old proudly placed Alaska and asked, "Mommy, is that heaven way up in the corner?" My two-year-old remarked while going to the bathroom, "Does Jesus have a potty?" I could tell you many more Williamson stories, but you don't need to hear the lead-ins to quiet times that my children share with me; every day your child gives you a dozen of your own.

The most important question then is: Are you ready and willing to create a meaningful quiet time when your child shows interest in talking about God? True devotions turn our attention away from ourselves and our earthly responsibilities. They empty center stage so that the spotlight is on Christ. A quiet time might be only long enough for a few words about scripture, for a song, or for a sentence prayer. Even in its brevity, a spontaneous quiet time with preschoolers shows them that we, like they, have Jesus in our thoughts.

In addition to such unplanned moments, we must have special times with our children when we set aside everything to come before God. Having regular devotions ourselves sets the stage for having special moments of devotions with our children. As with spontaneous worship, planned quiet times must focus on Christ. This is not something we do to prove that we are good or to insure that our children will be good. We have devotions because God is good, and God deserves our attention and praise.

When God's holiness becomes the focus of family devotions, the central point of Christianity is magnified: Christ died to redeem each of us from sin. Homes in which both parent and child acknowledge a dependence on God take on an atmosphere of mutual confession and praise. As Christian parents, we can be powerful witnesses. We are Christ's ambassadors. Being Christ's representative in the home is as significant as being a witness to our colleague in the office, our neighbor across the fence, or our physician. Yet, too often, we save only scraps of time and tidbits of creative energy for the spiritual nurture of our offspring during their most formative, preschool years.

To spark a child's interest we must allow the Holy Spirit to tend the fire of our own faith. The meditations in this chapter are meant to prepare you for leading children in worship by providing tinder and kindling for your own heart.

Opportunities for Sharing Christ with Your Child

The essence of a preschooler's quiet time is the quality time that the child spends with parents. Playtime blends into devotional time as parent and child turn their attention to God. Two minutes of directed thought out of ten minutes of play might be sufficient for your youngster. Place your emphasis on talking with God rather than on the teaching or the content of learning. When your child tells you, "Mommy, you owe me two devotions," you will know you're on the right track.

Don't always save your discussion for the end of a devotional activity. Learn to talk naturally about Jesus as you do other friends, and your child will learn how, too.

Consider each child's needs. Depending on the devotional activity and the age span of your children, you may wish to have devotions in a family group or with each child individually.

The things that held your child's interest this week may seem outdated next week. Look for ways to heighten variety and the element of surprise. Flexibility must compensate for a child's amazing growth rate. Make having devotions a family tradition, but vary the contents to meet your family's current needs.

Devotional Activities for the Preschool Years

For the first 12 months of your child's life, make *security* the focus of regular quiet times. Sing songs of praise to Jesus, read your Bible out loud, make happy conversation, and smile—because Jesus loves both you and your child.

From 12 months on, add *celebration.* Clap and sing, dance and raise hands in praise, enjoy picture books, and learn the name of Jesus.

During your child's third year, add *discovery.* Share finger plays, short contemporary stories that show God's love, simple Bible stories, short scripture verses, and the wonders of God's creation.

Beginning at age four, add *integrity*. As your child learns more about who Jesus is, help your child to grow in the awareness that we are responsible for our own actions. Teach your child that the Holy Spirit is God's presence with us and that Christians need the Spirit's indwelling to live successfully for God. Loving God is a choice, and being a Christian means saying no to selfish desires, accepting Christ's death and resurrection, and inviting God's control in life.

Ideas for Finding Time

Establish traditions that make bedtime, mealtime, and bathtime moments that include worship and talks about God. Sing to your child, read, or have quiet talks about God's blessings.

Establish times to pray together. Meals, snack times, and car trips are some of the times we've chosen.

Decide on a time for devotions, and play this game: Set the stove timer or listen for the strike-clock, if you have one, to signal the start of your time together. When the bell sounds, have everyone—parents and children alike—stop to spend a few minutes together with God. Do one of the devotional activities from this book. Make it a quality time, and soon your children will be asking for many repeats of this game. Leaving the dishes half done or the bills half paid to have devotions with your children demonstrates your commitment to putting God first.

Find the right weekly routine for your family. Perhaps start with one devotion on Sunday afternoon. Then add a new time such as a "Sunday School on Tuesday" session (see page 115) or a family night on Thursday that includes an activity and quiet time. Let children paste a foil star on the calendar each day you have a devotion, and see how many stars you can collect each month.

Don't overlook spontaneous moments for praise and talks with God. Lost socks, found puppies, thunderstorms, and rainbows all help to make conversations with God a natural part of family life.

Create in Me a Clean Heart

Bible Focus "But in your hearts set apart Christ as Lord" (1 Peter 3:15).

Meditation During a quiet time with my two preschoolers, I read Jesus' words, "I am the light of the world" (John 8:12). "Why did Jesus say that?" I asked. My three-year-old replied, "Because Jesus made the sun." My five-year-old said, "Because Jesus is king over everything, just like the sun shines over everything." Their answers provide insight into the development of a child's thoughts.

For most of their preschool years, children think concretely. Much of Scripture leaves them puzzled. "How can Jesus be light when he's a person?" preschoolers ask. Such analogies are beyond them. Little ones can, however, relate to God as the Creator of our world. They can understand Jesus in the context of the relationships they know: Jesus is loving, friendly, caring. For this reason, the way the parent lives and relates to others has lasting effects on the child's developing concept of God.

Apply the Bible focus verse to your relationship with your preschooler. Think in concrete terms. Has your day-to-day living reflected your hope in Christ? Does your preschooler know that you live for God? As parents, we have no choice but to be models for our children. Instead of pretending to be a perfect parent, however, it's better to work on being an honest one. Instead of justifying sin, confess it. Let your life, even the shortcomings in your life, provide a foundation for your child's understanding of Christ's love and his redemptive work.

Activity   Write a short letter to your child. In simple words, tell about your relationship with Jesus. Pray for a special time when you can read it to your child. Close your quiet time by praying from Psalm 51: "Create in me a pure heart, O God, and renew a steadfast spirit within me. Do not cast me from your presence or take your Holy Spirit from me. Restore to me the joy of your salvation and grant me a willing spirit, to sustain me" (vv. 10-12).

Making Introductions

Bible Focus   "You have not come to a mountain that can be touched and that is burning with fire. . . . But you have come to Mount Zion, to the heavenly Jerusalem" (Heb. 12:18, 22).

Meditation   As you prepare to have devotions with your preschooler, remember that you are not a philosopher passing on tenets to the next generation or a religionist drilling your novice on principles of faith. You are a believer who has gained access to the throne of God through the sacrifice of Christ. With your child you may daily enter into God's presence to worship God, to bring God honor, and to make your requests known. It is this privilege of access that motivates us to spend family time in worship and praise.

Devotions should be moments of discovery and celebration. Don't use quiet times for harsh disciplining. Picture yourself in the Lord's throne room, and know that your child is welcomed and accepted there even as you are. Jesus said, "Let the little children come to me, and do not hinder them, for the kingdom of heaven belongs to such as these" (Matt. 19:14). One of the most exciting aspects of having devotions with preschoolers is that the parent often has only the simple role of making introductions. Once children believe they are in the presence of a living, loving God, conversations with that God flow freely. As this happens in your home, your own faith will be stretched and strengthened by your child's simple faith.

Activity Listen to your child's ideas, interests, and possible reservations about having devotions. Share your interest in learning and worshiping *with* your child. Do an activity-oriented devotion together. Let your child have a say in scheduling your next quiet time. (Make sure you keep the promises you make.) Join hands with your child and pray: *Dear Lord, bless* (child's name) *as we begin having regular devotions together. Amen.*

Then lead your child in prayer: *Dear Lord, help* (Mommy/Daddy) *and me to have devotions together. Amen.*

Sowing Seeds of Righteousness

Bible Focus "Sow for yourselves righteousness, reap the fruit of unfailing love, and break up your unplowed ground; for it is time to seek the Lord" (Hos. 10:12).

Meditation For me, living with preschoolers is somewhat like traveling on a fast-moving train. Our family works, eats, and sleeps with only a muted awareness that we are racing forward on the tracks of time. Occasionally I glance out the window and realize we are not where we once were. There is no way of going back. Then, when it's too late, I regret that we didn't pause long enough to savor the territory we were passing through.

What occupies your time right now? Is it concern about house payments, job advancement, or bills? Though our children cannot fathom our preoccupations, they already are picking up on our priorities. What if we figure out a way to pay for their first single bed, their first dental checkup, and their first swimming lessons, and it leaves no time during the week for their father and mother to worship and pray? What if we manage to give them everything we think children should have, and neglect to give them reasons to cherish Christ?

Recommit yourself to Christ and to your children. Long to say with Paul: "I consider everything a loss compared to the surpassing greatness of knowing Christ Jesus my Lord, for whose sake I have lost all things. I consider them rubbish, that I may gain Christ" (Phil. 3:8). Memorize Prov. 14:26: "He who fears the Lord has a secure fortress, and for his children it will be a refuge."

Activity   Today sit down with your preschooler and look through your child's baby book. Tell your child how much you love him or her and how important he or she is to you. Later, when your little one is asleep, tiptoe to the bedside and pray: *Heavenly Father, help me to rely on your faithfulness. Be with me as I lead* (name your child) *in the walk of faith, so that* (he/she) *may know the fruit of your unfailing love. Amen.*

For a Limited Time Only

Bible Focus "I have been reminded of your sincere faith, which first lived in your grandmother Lois and in your mother Eunice and, I am persuaded, now lives in you also" (2 Tim. 1:5).

Meditation I attended a retreat where each woman shared her favorite photograph. It struck me later that many mothers displayed old pictures of their children as preschoolers. This brought home for me the fact that a family has its preschoolers for only a limited time.

We need to make time to explore the fascinating world of everyday with our preschoolers, because these days won't last forever. Times of active learning can enhance a child's mental and physical development. In a Christ-centered home these moments will also produce comfortable and rewarding times in which to talk about God. As Christian parents, we should not neglect having regular times of play with our children, for the family's sake and the church's sake as well. It seems likely that more Timothy-type young people might be found within our fellowships if more Lois- and Eunice-type grandparents and parents were found within our homes.

Are you willing to make your walks a little slower and your cleanup times a little longer for your child's sake? Are you willing to ask God for help in finding time to spend with your preschooler? As you reflect on these questions, remember—this offer comes to you for a limited time only.

Activity Begin a journal of your family's spiritual pilgrimage.

Pray this prayer: *Dear Father, help me to order my days so that I will have at least* (specify number) *hour(s) of play and active devotions each week with each of my children. Amen.*

Continue to pray for guidance, and make actual modifications in your daily routine until this prayer is answered.

Winning the Battle for Time

Bible Focus   "You shall not make for yourself an idol in the form of anything" (Exod. 20:4-6).

Meditation   When we eat dinner on the run, we tell our children that tonight's meeting is more important than tonight's meal. When we decide to drive to the corner store instead of walking there, we say that at the moment time is more important than exercise. Inevitably and often unknowingly, we communicate values to our children all day long by the simple choices we make concerning time.

The words of the Bible focus passage really hit home when we find ourselves saying, "We never seem to have time for family devotions." Most of us make time for television, working extra hours for extra pay, telephone conversations, and trips to the mall. If we neglect our devotional life, our children have a legitimate right to think these things are more important than our time with God.

Jesus said, "Store up for yourselves treasures in heaven. . . . For where your treasure is, there your heart will be also" (Matt. 6:19-21). Do we want our treasures to be in heaven? Do we truly want our children's treasures to be there too? Then let's start meeting with God, at any cost.

Activity   Look over the section, "Ideas for Finding Time" on page 10. Choose one or two suggestions to try this week. As you begin this adventure, share your thoughts with God in prayer.

The Transparent Prayer Closet

Bible Focus   "Be very careful, then, how you live—not as unwise but as wise, making the most of every opportunity" (Eph. 5:15).

Meditation   Have you started seeing yourself in your child? Is it the way she puts her little hand on her hip when she's upset, or the way he leans against the refrigerator during his telephone talks with Grandma? When our children imitate our actions it can be comical, endearing, or painfully revealing. Always it points to the truth that we serve as models for them.

Watch your child play. You'll see and hear what's been making an impression on him or her. Is your child reflecting an exposure to godly actions and speech? Some of our fondest family memories are of a two-year-old teaching a stuffed rabbit to pray and a three-year-old pretending to lead church hymns from his dining-room-chair pulpit and a four-year-old singing his own prayer songs while having a "quiet time" on his tricycle. Each was a reflection of times when we successfully made the most of an opportunity for personal or corporate worship.

Activity   Pray for wisdom that is sufficient to help you make the most of every opportunity with your child: *Lord, your Word says "Train a child in the way he should go, and when he is old he will not turn from it" (Prov. 22:6). Help me to provide loving, consistent training for* (child's name). *Amen.*

2

Every Day with God
Devotions for Children

I would strive to share my faith with my children, using informal settings and unplanned happenings. Rather than discuss abstract theology or impose rigid rules of family worship, I would pay more attention to the things my child notices and to what concerns him—and find in these a natural way to discuss spiritual truths.
— John M. Drescher, *If I Were Starting My Family Again*

Devotions can take place anytime and anywhere. Our Father in heaven desires us to draw near in the playroom as well as in the church pew. Including preschoolers in some of our moments of planned and spontaneous worship can increase our own excitement about spending time with God.

This chapter contains activity-oriented quiet times that revolve around common household objects. The devotions are designed to require little or no material preparation. Before you exhaust the ideas here, I'm sure you'll be making up new activities of your own. The conversational comments and questions used throughout the remainder of the book are for example only. Everywhere, you are encouraged to choose your own wording for activities. Though symbols on each page indicate an approximate age level and energy level for each devotion, your child's own personality and skills must be the final judges in deciding what activities are right for your quiet times.

Remember that *associations* are important to preschoolers. You want your shared quiet times to help your child make a happy association between personal devotions and the positive, loving moments your child shares with you. The time you spend together will also bring about a new selection of word and experience *association* that can hold great significance for your little one. The most exciting association to be made through preschooler-oriented devotions, however, comes when consistent quiet times show our children that Jesus is the consistent presence in our lives.

The following symbols will help you determine appropriate devotions to use with your child:

| Quiet | Moderate | Active |

The numbers in the box indicate an approximate age range. This, of course, will depend on the individual child.

Each quiet time also offers a Bible focus, a short section of Scripture that relates to or suggests a theme for the activity. The verse may trigger additional ideas for ways to share God's Word with the young members of your family. Always be open to the Holy Spirit's guiding presence in the devotional life of your little ones.

Hide and Seek

Bible Focus "[God] is not far from each one of us" (Acts 17:27).

Materials space for hide and seek, Bible

Activity Play hide and seek. With a very young child, play in teams with one parent and child hiding while the other parent seeks. Switch the roles of "hiders" and "seekers" until your child tires of the game. Then ask: "Was Jesus with us while we played hide and seek? Do you know that even when Daddy or Mommy can't see you, God knows right where you are?"

Point out the Bible focus verse in your Bible, and read it to your child. Explain how having God near you makes you feel safe. Share a short story of a time when you, as a Christian adult, called upon God to help you. Tell your child about the safe feelings you had knowing that God was near. At the end of your discussion, pray sentence-prayers of thanks for God's nearness.

Simon Says

Bible Focus   "Guide me in your truth and teach me, for you are God my Savior, and my hope is in you all day long" (Ps. 25:5).

Materials   Bible

Activity   Read the Bible focus verse from your Bible. Ask: "Do you want God to guide you? Do you want God to lead you? Mommy (Daddy) wants God's guidance. Any child or adult who does must learn to listen carefully to God. How can we listen to God? *(By reading the Bible, learning in Sunday school, praying, etc.)* Then as we listen, we must do as God says. How good a listener are you? Let's play a game to practice both listening and doing."

Explain the game: "When I say 'Simon says,' you follow my instructions. But when I don't say 'Simon says,' you don't follow my instruction."

Play several rounds of the game, using mistakes as gentle reminders that good followers must be good listeners. Then let each child take a turn at being the leader. By your actions show that parents, too, must listen carefully when instructions are given.

After the game, read the Bible focus verse again. Discuss ideas generated by the game: Listening and following aren't easy; sometimes we make mistakes even when we don't want to; doing better comes with practice; etc. Then challenge each player to go through the day thinking about "Jesus says." When "Jesus says" we should do something, we should do it. At the same time we should stay away from doing things that Jesus would say no to.

Pray for each other, and remember to let your child pray for you also: *Dear God, I pray that you will help* (name) *to follow you today. Amen.*

Extra-special idea As your child learns verses that contain Jesus' words, try playing "Jesus says." Read or recite verses. Have your child raise a hand whenever words of Jesus are read.

Made from the Dust

Bible Focus "And the Lord God formed man from the dust of the ground and breathed into his nostrils the breath of life, and man became a living being" (Gen. 2:7).

Materials clay or playdough (to make, see recipe below), Bible

Activity Enjoy creating your own animals. Begin by making a new batch of playdough:

Mix together in a medium saucepan: 1 cup flour, ¼ cup salt, and 2 tablespoons cream of tartar. Stir together in a separate bowl: 1 cup water, 1 teaspoon food coloring (whatever color is desired), and 1 tablespoon cooking oil. Add to dry mixture, and stir over medium heat for 3 to 5 minutes. The goo will thicken in the center of the pan first, and as you continue to stir, a soft ball will form. (The suspense of waiting for this to happen is part of the fun.) Spoon the dough onto a lightly floured surface. Make sure it is cool enough to handle, and knead until it is the consistency of commercially prepared playdough. Store in an airtight container.

Using the playdough, make both imaginary creatures and copies of real animals. Pretend that they are alive and can eat, drink, and move.

Toward the end of your playtime, ask your child how the first human being on earth was made. Read the Bible focus verse, and emphasize how God carefully and lovingly formed humans from the dust of the earth. Using playdough, have your child act out the story. Stress that only the breath of the Creator-God can change clay into a living being.

Before cleanup, hold your child's doughy hands and pray: *Lord, we know you are very great. You made the first person from the dust of the earth. Thank you for life. Amen.*

Help your child to say: *Thank you, God, for giving me life. Amen.*

Trust Walks

Bible Focus "Do not let your hearts be troubled and do not be afraid" (John 14:27).

Materials blindfold, Bible

Activity Explore your backyard or another familiar place by taking a trust walk. Blindfold your child and then take his or her hand. Then find things to smell, feel, and hear. Continue the activity until you know your child feels at ease. Talk about how gentle words and steady hands can give direction and protection.

After the activity, talk about your trust walk. Ask: "Were you afraid on the walk? Did you trust my help and guidance? When we trust the person who is guiding us, we don't have to be afraid."

Then read Jesus' words in the Bible focus verse. Ask: "Why does Jesus tell us not to be afraid?" *(Because Jesus wants us to have his peace. Because he's right beside us every minute of the day and night.)* Talk about some things that are scary for you and for your child. Decide that the next time you feel fear you will try to picture Jesus holding your hand and leading you on a trust walk through that scary time.

Pray and tell Jesus that you want to be able to trust in him. Ask for his help in overcoming specific fears.

Important Signposts

Bible Focus   "Write them on the doorframes of your houses and on your gates" (Deut. 6:9).

Materials   crayons or felt-tipped markers, paper or poster board, masking tape, Bible

Activity   Read the entire Bible focus passage (Deut. 6:5-9). Ask: "Why did God know it was important for the Chosen People, the Israelites, to think about God's commandments when they got up in the morning, and when they walked and talked together, and when they went to bed? *(Share your own answer to this question.)* Have you thought about God today?"

Suggest that you make some sort of reminder to put on each outside door in your home. Write "Love the Lord" on each poster, but let your child do the artwork. Your child will probably want you to do some signs too. When the "signs" are finished, tape one to the inside of each exit door.

Whenever someone in your family or a visitor is ready to leave, say, "Remember, Jesus loves you. Go with God." As long as the reminders are on the doors, try praying together as a family before going out at the start of each day: *Heavenly Father, as we leave our home now, guide us according to your gracious will. Amen.*

Hiding behind Masks

Bible Focus "Lord, you know everyone's heart" (Acts 1:24).

Materials paper plates, string, crayons or felt-tipped markers, scissors, Bible

Activity Help your child to make a paper plate mask. Have each participating family member make one. Cut eye holes and add string ties so that the masks can be worn. Add to the fun of trying to disguise yourself by trading masks and pretending that you are another member of the family. As you make the masks, discuss how God made each of us special. God doesn't want us to be anyone else. Even when we are bad or sad, God cares how we feel. Sometimes we try to hide our feelings, but God knows what we are thinking inside.

Read the Bible focus verse from your Bible. Then write the following poem on each mask. Let your child suggest different feelings—sadness, anger, fear, etc.—to be named.

Sometimes my feelings I try to hide *(Write on the outside plate rim).*

. . . but God knows what I'm really thinking inside. *(Write on the inside plate rim).*

Keep your masks as a reminder of this lesson. Pray together this prayer: *Thank you, God, that you always know where I am. Thank you, God, that you always know how I feel. Amen.*

My New Song to God

Bible Focus "I will sing a new song to you, O God" (Ps. 144:9).

Materials Bible, real or spur-of-the-moment instruments such as pie plates, spoons, salt box drums, etc.

Activity Open your Bible and read aloud the Bible focus verse. Share these thoughts: Long ago David showed his love to God by making up new songs to sing praises to God. Sometimes David sang his songs directly to God. Sometimes he shared them with others so that those who heard could praise God, too. Ask: "Do you think we can make up a new song of praise to sing to God?" Let your child suggest words and music. Try your child's suggestion or use one of the following ideas:

Use the name of every family member and sing a new song to the tune of "The Farmer in the Dell":

> Oh, Jesus loves (child's name)
> Oh, yes, he loves him (her) so.
> And that is why I sing this song
> Just so you all will know.

Sing "God Is So Good" and add this additional verse. Point to each item as you sing.

> God made the sky,
> God made the trees,
> God made the flowers,
> he's so good to me.

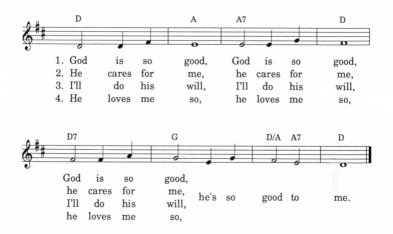

For your baby or child, collect safe noise makers from the kitchen and elsewhere. Read the rest of Ps. 144:9: ". . . on the ten-stringed lyre I will make music to you." Create your own instruments. Let your child sing his or her own words and make noises of joyful praise. Participate in the songs.

Wrap up your time by pointing out that singing is one way of saying thanks to God. Put your instruments away. Then quietly pray: *Thank you for music, God. Thank you that we can make up new songs for you. Amen.*

Extra-special music ideas

■ Help your child to record music on an easy-to-use, durable tape recorder. Share the tape with an elderly or homebound person or with a friend who is ill.

■ Sing hymns or songs of praise each day as you care for your infant. By doing so, you surround the child with an atmosphere of peace and cheer. Give rattles and simple instruments to an active baby; he or she will enjoy making a "joyful noise." Continue to sing as your child grows. Let car trips, walks, and bathtime be traditional times for song.

■ Clap and dance to the songs you sing, or do this type of "active listening" in response to a praise record or tape.

■ "Play the old jukebox." Have your child pretend to put a penny into a slot (your pocket) and press a button (your nose). Sing whatever song your child selects. Request songs from your child, too. Play this game while traveling.

How Many Hairs on Your Head?

Bible Focus   "Indeed, the very hairs of your head are all numbered" (Luke 12:7).

Materials   mirror, Bible

Activity   Stand in front of a mirror and try counting the hairs on your child's head. When you and your child give up the count, ask: "Do you think anyone could know how many hairs are on your head?" Open your Bible and read the Bible focus verse. Ask: "Do you believe Jesus' words? How does it make you feel to know that God looks after you so closely that God knows exactly how many hairs are on your head?" Let your child share his or her thoughts. Then share your own feelings about a God who knows everything about you and cares for you personally.

Pray a prayer of thanks for God's love and care. Help your child to bring special health and safety needs before God through prayer.

Extra-special bedtime idea   Count your blessings. Some night when your child can't sleep take him or her into your arms. Quietly list and talk about God's blessings. Name them one by one until your child falls asleep. Then tuck your child into bed, and thank God in prayer for the precious gifts you have received.

How Many Are Your Works

Bible Focus "How many are your works, O LORD! In wisdom you made them all" (Ps. 104:24).

Materials buttons or pennies, Bible

Activity From age two on, a child becomes increasingly interested in numbers and counting. Encourage counting activities by counting out things you see around you during the day, such as the trees in your backyard, the places set at the dinner table, or the number of fingers and toes on your child. Talk about things in the Bible that can be counted and things too many to count, such as the stars in the sky, the individual blades of grass in a field, or the number of grains of sand on the beach. Play a counting game with the buttons or pennies. Count out a specific number and tell a Bible story about it. You might tell the story of Jesus choosing the 12 disciples (Luke 6:12-16), or the feeding of the throng with five loaves and two fish (John 6:1-13).

Close your quiet time by reading the Bible focus verse and talking about how many, many things God gives us and does for us. Pray together: *Dear God, your works are many! Though I like to count, I cannot count them all! Thank you, Lord, for loving us so much. Amen.*

Built on a Rock

Bible Focus   "He is like a man building a house, who dug down deep and laid the foundation on rock" (Luke 6:48).

Materials   wooden or plastic building blocks, pillow, Bible

Activity   Read the story of the two builders from Luke 6:47-49. Then tell your child that you are going to act out the story by building two houses with blocks. Build the first house on top of a pillow, making it high enough so that it will topple from the unstable surface. Then, together build a second house on a firm surface, such as a table top or tile floor. Talk about how much stronger this house is. It will not topple easily because it has been built on a firm foundation.

Explain that Jesus was talking about faith in the story he told. If we place our faith in Jesus, we are building on a firm foundation, and our faith will hold strong when faced with troubles, just as the wise builder's house held strong in the storm.

Close your quiet time together by praying: *Thank you, Jesus, for giving us a foundation we can build upon. You will hold us strong and fast. We love you. Amen.*

Extra-special building-block talks

■ Read from a child's Bible the story of Nehemiah work to repair the walls around Jerusalem (Neh. 2:11—3:32) or tell the story in simple language. Then pretend you are building that wall, using toy figures and blocks.

Include as much of the drama as possible—the need for families to build their part of the wall in their own backyards, the constant threat of attack, the raising of the heavy gates, etc. Point out the need for cooperation in that project and in the projects that you face today.

■ Lay your own cornerstone and then build a church on top of it. Talk about the concepts in the "Looking for Cornerstones" on page 75.

■ Act out the story of Joshua and the walls of Jericho (Josh. 6:1-20). Read the story from a children's Bible or retell it in simple language. Build a wall of blocks, march around it seven times, shout, and knock it down. Talk about how Joshua and the people had to have faith in God. They had to believe that God would take down the walls.

The Gratefulness Game

Bible Focus "Give thanks in all circumstances, for this is God's will for you in Christ Jesus" (1 Thess. 5:18).

Setting a long car trip or some other situation where a thinking game is welcomed

Activity Play the "Gratefulness Game" by taking turns mentioning things for which you are thankful. For a young child, the rules can be as simple as naming things you see from the car window: I am thankful for trees, water, cows, corn, etc. With a child who is learning the alphabet, try making an "I am thankful for . . ." list that includes every letter.

Practice distinguishing letter sounds by giving a set of challenges that includes naming something you're thankful for that begins with "ch," with "c," etc. Use colors or textures or sounds as the categories and name something you're thankful for that is blue, that is soft, that is loud, and so forth.

Don't worry if some answers are silly ones. Make it a fun game. Then give thanks to God for the opportunity to have a good time: *God, we have so many things for which we are thankful. Thank you for this time to think about some of them. Amen.*

The Creator

Bible Focus "Remember your Creator . . ." (Eccles. 12:1).

Materials finger paints and finger paint paper or "pudding paint" and aluminum foil, Bible

Activity Play with conventional finger paints, or make "pudding paint" (one three-ounce box of instant pudding mixed with 2½ cups of milk) so your child can make edible pictures on a large sheet of aluminum foil.

Compliment your child on his or her completed project. Talk about the meaning of the word *creator*. Ask: "Who is the creator of this artwork? (*The child.*) I like your picture; you are a good picture creator." Then read the Bible focus verse from your Bible. Say: "The Bible tells us to remember our Creator. Who is our Creator? (*God*) A creator is someone who designs and makes a project. God designed us and made us. That's why we call God our Creator. You designed your picture and made it. That's why I can call you a picture creator. When I look at your picture, I see what you have made. But you created only the picture. God created the aluminum and the cow that made milk and all the stuff that is in the pudding. And God created you and me too! When I look at you and at the wonderful world outside, I see what God has made." Talk about the wonders that our Creator has made, and end your conversation by praying: *Thank you, God, for making me. You are my Creator, and I love you very much. Amen.*

The Lost Sheep

Bible Focus "If a man owns a hundred sheep, and one of them wanders away, will he not leave the ninety-nine on the hills and go to look for the one that wandered off?" (Matt. 18:12).

Materials a toy sheep (hidden before the devotion starts), Bible

Activity Read the Bible focus verse and explain that this is the beginning of a story that Jesus told to his disciples. Point out the important parts of this verse: "A man has many, many sheep, but one of them gets lost. What does the man do? Does he forget about that one poor lonely sheep or does he go looking for it?" *(He leaves all the others, and he goes to look for the one lost sheep.)*

Have your child look for the "lost" sheep that you have already hidden. When the sheep is found, talk about the story again. Then explain that the Bible calls us Jesus' sheep. No matter where we go, God is near us. Even when we feel scared or alone, we can believe that God is with us. God cares about us as much as the man in Jesus' story cared about his sheep. Even though he had 99 of his sheep, he still went looking for the one that got lost. Pray together, thanking God for loving us and caring for us.

Finger Friends

Bible Focus "Remember the wonders [God] has done" (1 Chron. 16:12).

Materials homemade finger puppets (see page 43), Bible

Activity Read the Bible focus verse. Talk about some of God's great works in the Bible. Choose a story from the Old or New Testament, and act it out with finger puppets. Here are some good stories to start with:

The Wise Men visit Jesus (Matt. 2:1-12): Make a Herod puppet for your left hand and some Wise Men puppets for your right hand. Have the Wise Men come and talk with Herod on their search for Jesus. Then replace Herod with puppets of Jesus, Mary, and Joseph. Have the Wise Men follow the star, bow before Jesus, give gifts and leave by a safe route.

Jesus calls his followers: Make a Jesus puppet and some disciple puppets. You can even put disciples in fishing boats or behind tax desks by using props made from paper strips taped together. Read Mark 1:16-20, Mark 2:13-14, and John 1:43-51. Act out how Jesus called his disciples. Then share the story of how Jesus calls us to follow him.

Puppets of any kind can help children express their real feelings. For a special time of sharing, have your puppet and your child's puppet "talk together" about a common fear or frustration. Be a good listener, and encourage your child's puppet to "talk about its feelings."

Ways to Make Finger Puppets

■ Use a fine-tipped, washable watercolor pen to draw faces directly onto your fingers.

■ Use open-ended peanut shells, small cosmetic bottle lids, or thimbles. Draw the facial features on one part of the surface and decorate with scraps of fabric and paper.

■ Cut out family faces from surplus snapshots and glue each one onto a small paper ring or attach to a craft stick. Use these personalized puppets for skits about your own family.

■ Cut out small animal and people figures from magazines and Sunday school take-home papers. Leave an inch by half-inch tab at the base of each cutout. Bend the tabs around and tape to form a finger ring that will fit firmly on little fingers.

■ Cut off knitted fingers from old gloves and sew on faces and clothes.

Act-It-Out

Bible Focus "We will tell the next generation the praiseworthy deeds of the Lord, his power, and the wonders he has done" (Ps. 78:4).

Materials simple dress-up clothes and props

Activity Act out a Bible story. Even simple, minute-long dramas can make a lasting impression on your child. Take advantage of spontaneous opportunities for drama that can "tell the next generation the praiseworthy deeds of the Lord." For example, our two-year-old decided to play "baby Jesus in the manger" by climbing into the suitcase I was unpacking after a Christmastime vacation. His imagination and interest in the Christmas story delayed my housecleaning, but his actions gave me a precious opportunity to hear his perceptions of Christ's birth.

When your child wants to play "make-believe," go along. When acting out Bible-related situations, use questions to direct the child's thoughts, but don't dictate the moves. Join your child's world of imagination. Encourage imaginative play by providing simple props (boxes, old clothes, blankets, etc.). Then give your child the time and space needed to act out make-believe ideas.

Here are some easy "act-it-out" ideas:

■ Play shepherd and sheep. Use the parable from Matt. 18:12-14 to set the stage for action. Cuddle your "lost sheep" and say how happy you are to have him or her in your arms.

■ Act out the sower and the seed (Matthew 13). First be the sower. Then show how the seed grew in each type of soil by acting out each type of plant mentioned.

■ Show each passerby's reaction to the injured man in the story of the good Samaritan (Luke 10:25-37).

■ Be blind Bartimaeus. Take his words and actions from the account in Mark 10:46-52. Blindfold your child so he or she feels blindness.

■ Act out a story with a familiar Bible character such as Noah or Moses. Have family members guess the character's identity.

Simple, planned family dramas can be a fun alternative to television. Invite another family with preschoolers to your home. Do short skits based on Bible stories. Serve light refreshments and close the evening with a short time of prayer.

Real or Unreal?

Bible Focus "So we fix our eyes not on what is seen, but on what is unseen" (2 Cor. 4:18).

Materials television

Activity Watch television with your child. Be sensitive to the fact that young children can have a hard time separating reality from unreality. Help your child to learn that TV carries "unspoken messages" as well as programs and commercials. Here are some ideas:

■ "Is that real?" This is a good first question for children two and older. Ask this question as you watch the action in a comic-hero program. Later, use your TV time as the seed for devotions. Read the Christmas story in Luke 1 and 2, Peter's miraculous escape from prison in Acts 12, or one of the many other accounts of God's intervention. Show how our real God is stronger, wiser, and more just than the pretend TV hero. Point out that the real heros in this world are those who live for God and show both God's strength and God's love. Then pray for a personal desire to be as strong and brave as God's most faithful followers.

■ "What are the TV ads trying to tell me?" Help your older preschool child see how some ads can fool us into believing that happiness comes from a pair of jeans or a cereal box. Talk about how belief in Jesus Christ is the way to find real joy. Work toward contentment in your own home by thanking God for the things you have.

■ "How many things to want and to buy?" Write down each tempting thing advertised during one regular Saturday morning or evening of television watching. Then read the list out loud. Count the items. Talk about your family's real needs. Decide if your wants and your plans are in line with God's will. As a family memorize the Bible focus verse. Make a plaque to display this verse on top of your TV set, so that the words can speak to you as you watch television.

■ When television seems in direct competition for time that could be spent in family activities or devotions, cut down on viewing time. Plan your TV watching. At the beginning of the week, go through your local TV schedule and mark which shows you will watch. Avoid impulsive watching. Talk about the reasons for choosing the programs you selected. Then write down a list of activities you plan to substitute for TV viewing. Children learn by example. Parents need to change their own TV habits, too.

■ Encourage discussion as you watch a program. Is what you are seeing real or not real? Are the values portrayed those we should imitate? Talk about how artists and writers can stretch our thinking in both good ways and bad ways. Expose your children to videos that show how television can be used to share the good news of Christ.

■ Try something new by having a "no television" night, weekend or week. Find creative activities to do in place of watching TV. Then thank God for the fun family time you had. Or check with your Christian bookstore for helps in the wise use of television and for a listing of Christ-centered videotapes. Use these resources to create special recreational events for your family. Close each activity with a short time of prayer.

Cling to the Good

Bible Focus "Love must be sincere. Hate what is evil; cling to what is good" (Rom. 12:9).

Materials magnets, Bible

Activity Show how magnets will cling to only certain, special metals. Go around your house looking for surfaces to which the magnets will cling. Does the refrigerator have these special metals? The light post? The door knob? Read the Bible focus verse. Ask: "What are Christians supposed to cling to? Name some good things (being truthful, being patient, serving others, etc.). Talk about the need to "cling" to these things. Above all, talk about how we need to cling to God and to God's merciful love.

Pray by holding hands and having each person make a sentence prayer: Help us, Lord, to cling to (name a good trait) as a way of showing that we love you. Amen.

Be Wise

Bible Focus   "I will give you a wise and discerning heart" (1 Kings 3:12).

Materials   two different boxes of breakfast cereal with the contents exchanged

Activity   Let your child choose a cereal based on the information and picture on the outside of the boxes. Dump the contents into a bowl and wait for your child's surprised reaction. Ask: "What does it feel like to be fooled by getting something different from what you expected?" Discuss the dangers of making choices based only on outward appearances. Use familiar situations: a toy car that looks strong but breaks quickly because it is made from weak plastic, a game that looks easy but is hard to play, etc.

Tell your child that to make good choices we need to see all parts of a decision. We need to be wise and discerning, as the Bible says. Look up the Bible focus verse and read it aloud. Say: "Being wise and discerning is difficult, but God can help us. King Solomon learned that. He asked God for a wise and discerning heart, and God gave him his request. Do you want a wise and discerning heart? I do, because making good choices is an important part of learning to follow Jesus."

Conclude by reading the Bible focus verse again and praying: *Lord, please make me able to see and choose what is right. Give me a wise and discerning heart. Amen.*

Taken for Granted

Bible Focus "Praise the Lord, O my soul, and forget not all his benefits" (Ps. 103:2).

Materials valve to turn off water in your home, paper and pencil, Bible

Activity Gather around the kitchen table for devotions. Begin by asking: "Do you know what it means to take something for granted? It means that we get so used to having something important that we start forgetting to be thankful for it. We can take a lot of things for granted—our food, our house, our family. *(Go to the kitchen sink.)* Do you take water for granted? *(Turn on the faucet and let the water run. Have the valve closed so that the faucet soon runs dry.)* What if we couldn't get any more water in the sink? Then we'd remember how important water really is, and we'd be grateful for it, wouldn't we?"

Show your child how to restore water to the faucet. Then read the Bible focus verse. Talk about these questions: Do we take God's love for granted? Do we get so used to living in a Christian family that we forget to be thankful to God and to each other? Have your child help you to put the Bible focus verse into words that are meaningful to your family. List on the paper some of God's "benefits" in your everyday life. Post your list. Pray and thank God for each one on your list. Then sing a song of praise together.

Tea Party with Jesus

Bible Focus   "Share with God's people who are in need. Practice hospitality" (Rom. 12:13).

Materials   dolls, stuffed animals, and supplies for a pretend tea party

Activity   Help your child set up a tea party. Invite dolls and animals, prepare food, and set the table. Make all the visitors feel special and welcome.

Before you eat, help your child say grace at the table. After the party, help your child put everything away. Point out that having guests in your home and serving them food takes work and planning. Say that today you practiced hospitality with the animals and dolls. Read the Bible focus verse and talk about how God wants us to practice hospitality to everyone to show our love for Christ. God tells us to share with those in need.

Think of someone in your church who doesn't usually get invited out for a meal. With your child's help, make a dinner invitation for that person. (Later, take your child along to deliver the invitation.) Close your devotion time together with this prayer: *Lord, help us to make someone happy this week by our willingness to practice hospitality. Help us to share with people in need. Amen.*

The Grocery Store

Bible Focus   "His divine power has given us everything we need for life and godliness" (2 Peter 1:3).

Materials   a grocery list

Activity   With your child's help, make a grocery list. Then go to the store and buy what is on your list. Your child can help you find coupon items by matching the pictures on the coupons with the products on the shelves. As you unpack the groceries at home, talk about how food and clothes are only part of what we need to be happy or content in life. Make a list of important things—such as love, peace, joy, patience, etc.—that cannot be bought in stores. Ask your child where you can get these important things. Test out the answer "from Jesus" by going down your list and talking about the promises Jesus has made concerning love, peace, joy, and patience.

Read the Bible focus verse. Talk about its promise. Then share how you go to God in prayer to ask for God's love, peace, and joy in specific situations. See what needs your child has, and go to God in prayer: *Heavenly Father, you know our need for* (name specific request). *We believe you are able to supply this need. We thank you that we can talk to you. We thank you that you will give us everything that we need. Amen.*

Neighbors

Bible Focus   "Love your neighbor as yourself" (Mark 12:31).

Materials   ingredients for a batch of cookies, or materials with which to make a card (paper, crayons, etc.), Bible

Activity   Read the Bible focus verse. Also read verse 30. Talk about Jesus' words that say we should love God and our neighbors. Think about the neighbors you know and talk about their needs. Is someone sick? Is someone lonely? Does someone have a new baby? Is it someone's birthday? Make a simple gift to match one neighbor's need.

If you do not know of any neighbor's specific needs, make a plate of cookies, put together a basket of fruit, or design a homemade card as a way of getting to know a neighbor better. With your child, deliver the gift personally. If the opportunity presents itself, explain that your gift of friendship is an outgrowth of the fun times you have studying God's Word together. After you return from your visit, take time to pray for your neighbor.

First Baby Stories

Bible Focus "[Mary] wrapped [Jesus] in cloths and placed him in a manger, because there was no room for them in the inn" (Luke 2:7).

Materials pictures of Jesus' birth from Christmas cards, Sunday school leaflets, or Bible storybooks and family photos taken when your child was born

Activity Share photographs or family stories of events surrounding your child's birth: What happened the day he or she was born? Where was your child born? What happy things do you remember about the moment of the birth? What happened right after the birth? Who came to visit first?

Then talk about the familiar story of Jesus' birth. Ask the same questions about Jesus' birth that you used when reviewing your child's birth. Answer any questions your child has about his or her own birth, the birth of Jesus, or the birth of babies in general. Be prepared to share some simple information about the wonderful experience of seeing a baby born.

At the end of your discussion pray together: *Lord Jesus, I thank you that you were born. I'm glad I know about your first baby stories from my Bible. I'm glad you know my baby stories, too. I love you. Amen.*

The Family Gift Box

Bible Focus "Therefore, as we have opportunity, let us do good to all people" (Gal. 6:10).

Materials a gift-wrapped box with a slit in the top and slips of paper

Activity Read the Bible focus verse. Explain to your child that we can give each other different kinds of gifts, but the most important presents we can give are ones that truly show love and care. Often, kind actions make better gifts than the ones we buy.

Show your child the gift-wrapped box. Say: "Sometimes it's hard to think of kindness as a gift. But a Family Gift Box like this one can help us see what kinds of good things we are doing for each other. Whenever you see someone do something good for someone else in our family, I'll help you write down that person's deed on a piece of paper that you can drop into the box. And, when you do something helpful or kind, I'll write it down. Let's see how many slips of paper we can collect today."

At the end of the day, count the number of slips you have collected. Talk about some of the good deeds that brought help and joy to your family. Build up each person who participated by sharing positive comments and words of praise. Read the Bible focus verse again and pray: Lord, thank you for this family. We love you and we love each other. Help us to get better and better at finding opportunities to do kind things for one another. Amen.

Names

Bible Focus   "You are to give him the name Jesus, because he will save his people from their sins" (Matt. 1:21).

Materials   Bible, pencil and paper (optional)

Activity   Read the Bible focus verse. Talk about how the angel told Joseph what to name Mary's baby. Explain that *Jesus* means "the Lord saves." Ask why that is a good name for this special baby.

Tell your child about his or her own name. Did you choose it for a special reason? Does your child have a nickname that shows something special about him or her? Tell what you know about your own name or names of others in your family. If you wish, write out the names as you talk so that your preschooler can see the letters in them.

Then ask: "Do you think Jesus knows your name?" Read John 10:3-11. Then say, "Jesus says he is the good shepherd who takes care of his sheep—his people. In verse 3 Jesus says that he calls his own sheep by name."

Pray together: *Thank you, God, that I have a name and that you know who I am. Amen.*

Reflections

Bible Focus "And we . . . reflect the Lord's glory" (2 Cor. 3:18).

Materials a mirror and small, heart-shaped pieces of aluminum foil

Activity Ask: "What is a reflection? *(Look into the mirror.)* A mirror makes a reflection. When we look into it, a mirror reflects our face. *(Hold the mirror so that you can see the other person's reflection.)* I can see your reflection in the mirror. Can you see mine?"

Read the Bible focus verse and talk about it. Explain that we can reflect God's glory so that other people can see what God is like. When we love we reflect God's love. When we show joy we reflect God's joy. God's Spirit is in us to help us be a reflection of the Lord.

Talk about how we often forget that we are to be a reflection of God. Give your child the small foil hearts. Say: "Here are some shiny hearts. They can remind us of little mirrors. When I say 'go,' run and hide your hearts in places where I will find them. I'll hide some in places where you will find them." (This activity is most joyful when family members work in teams. When you are finished hiding the hearts, pray: *Thank you, God, for the fun of hurrying around and hiding hearts. Every time we find one, Lord, let it remind us to be a reflection of you. Amen.*

Whenever a family member finds a heart in the days to come, have him or her call out "I will be a reflection of God." During a meal, talk about where hearts were found and how finding them made you feel.

Important Letters

Bible Focus   "I, Paul, write this greeting in my own hand" (1 Cor. 16:21).

Materials   letters from your mailbox, Bible

Activity   Let your child get the mail from your box. Go through it, and read aloud all or part of a letter from a friend. Talk about why your friend wrote a letter. Explain that much of the New Testament is made up of letters written between Christian friends. Read the Bible focus verse as an example that explains who wrote the Bible letters. Find other places where Paul says he is writing the words himself or telling a scribe (someone like a secretary) what words to write.

Flip through some of Paul's letters and the letters of James, Peter, and John to show your child the Bible letters. Ask: "Why did Paul, James, Peter, and other early Christians write letters?" *(To tell others about Jesus, to teach other Christians how to live the Christian life, to encourage new churches.)* Thank God in prayer that these early letters have been saved in the Bible so that they can be read today.

Extra-special letter idea   Help your child write a letter to a friend or relative, telling that person what Jesus' love means to him or her. Read the message back to your child. Then help him or her decorate the letter, stamp it, and put it in the mailbox. Pray together at the mailbox that the letter will help someone else to believe in Christ.

Repent!

Bible Focus "Repent, then, and turn to God" (Acts 3:19).

Materials large sheet of paper, crayons, toy cars and trucks

Activity Read the Bible focus verse. Ask your child what he or she thinks the word *repent* means. Tell your child that you have a fun way to show the meaning of the word.

With your child, draw a series of intersections and roads on the large sheet of paper. Put in stop signs, parking lots, and destinations such as your house, your grocery store, your place of business, etc. Then drive the toy cars and trucks on the roads you've made. Play a game in which you drive a lead car and your child must follow to a certain place on the drawing. Then let your child lead, but as he or she does, follow poorly and make many wrong turns.

When your child complains about your wrong turns, remind your child that you wanted to talk about what it means to repent while playing this game. Tell your child to call out "Repent!" the next time you make a wrong turn. When he or she does this, go back and make the correct turn. Then explain that the word *repent* can mean going back to the point where you made a wrong turn and choosing the right way. Say that you can repent in real life as well as in this sort of game.

Stop your game long enough to tell how you repented in your own life. Tell what "wrong turns" you had taken (living to please self instead of God, etc.) and how you went back to those turns and chose instead to follow Christ. Mention that you still must repent when you choose ways that do not follow God's leading. Assure your child that God is ready to forgive us. Read the Bible focus verse again.

Pray together: *Lord, forgive us for choosing to do things that are different from what you would have us do. Lead us, Lord, and guide us today. Amen.*

(Continue to play cars with your child after your devotional period is over, so that your child knows you enjoy spending time together.)

Loving Jesus Most of All | 3-5

Bible Focus "I love the LORD" (Ps. 116:1).

Materials poster board, felt-tipped markers, and scissors

Activity Before beginning your quiet time, draw a puzzle outline on the poster board (see diagram on next page). Leave the puzzle pieces blank, and do not cut them apart. You will do this during the quiet time.

Read the Bible focus verse out loud. Talk about the need to put Jesus first in your life, to love him more than anything else. Then show the blank puzzle. Ask your child or each participating family member to name some things that are important in life. Write one of these responses—a nice house, food to eat, a job, etc.—on each of the edge pieces. Let your child draw appropriate pictures on each piece. Write "Loving Jesus" on the center heart. Tell your child that you hope he or she will always make "Loving Jesus" the most important part of living. Once all the pieces are filled in, cut the puzzle apart.

Have your child close his or her eyes while you hide the puzzle pieces around the room. Put the "Loving Jesus" heart aside so that it cannot be found. Then have your child look for the puzzle pieces. As your child puts the puzzle back together, talk about how this puzzle shows many important things in life. It shows a nice house, food to eat, a good job, etc. Then ask: "But what piece is missing?" *(The "Loving Jesus" part.)* Give the missing heart to your child, and let your child complete the puzzle by putting it in the center. Read the Bible focus verse again. Conclude your quiet time by talking about how a person needs Jesus to make his or her life complete.

Ask for a show of hands on who is willing to put "Loving Jesus" at the center of his or her life. Then close in prayer: *Dear heavenly Father, we want loving Jesus to be the most important part of our lives today and every day. Amen.*

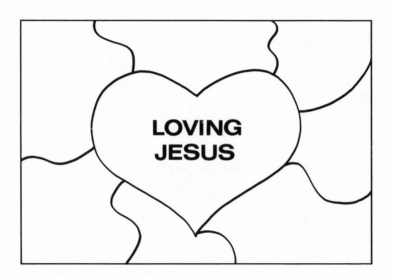

New Every Morning

Bible Focus "For his compassions [kindnesses] never fail. They are new every morning" (Lam. 3:22-23).

Materials seven small gifts such as pocket-size Bible storybooks, magic capsules that change into Bible symbols when put into warm water, erasers with verses printed on them, etc.

Activity Wrap seven small gifts and place them in a basket. Each morning for a week have your child choose a gift. Be prepared to have a short devotion based on the gift for that day. *(Read the book, talk about the scripture on the eraser, etc.)* Then say the Bible focus verse together. By the end of the week you should have it memorized. Talk about your own feelings of joy and expectation that come from knowing that God's mercies are new each morning. Talk with your child about God's constant love and care. Explain that the little gifts in the basket are to remind your child of the big, unseen gifts that come every day as God watches over and cares for your family. Thank God for God's mercy today, and every day.

Extra-special idea Use this grab-bag approach to daily devotions on a week when waiting is hard or when your child is sick or in the hospital. Or help your child make "New Every Morning" surprises for a Sunday school teacher's birthday or for a sick friend.

The Lord's Work

Bible Focus   "Whatever you do, work at it with all your heart, as working for the Lord" (Col. 3:23).

Materials   housekeeping items and toys

Activity   Play house with your child. Clean, cook, baby-sit, or do whatever activities your child chooses. Talk about the jobs you like doing and the ones you don't like doing, but do them all cheerfully.

Point out that running a house takes lots of work. Name as many jobs as you can think of. Make sure your preschooler feels he or she can contribute to the real family household by having at least one small responsibility (such as putting silverware into the dishwasher or hanging up his or her own coat). Talk about the joys of having everyone help with the work. Admit that there will always be jobs that are not fun to do. Name some specific things that you do not like doing. Read the Bible focus verse. Tell your child how it helps to know that God cares when we have work that we don't like doing. Talk about how the verse tells us to do our best in everything, as though we were doing the work for Jesus.

With your child, do a simple household task, such as unloading the dryer or dusting furniture. Allow your child to take part in the work. Or pretend to do a job while playing house. Before you begin, pray: *Dear Father in heaven, we know this work needs to be done. Help us to do our job happily, knowing that you want us to do it well. Amen.*

After the job is done, thank your child for the completed work.

The Scribble Game

Bible Focus   "A happy heart makes the face cheerful" (Prov. 15:13).

Materials   paper and pencil or crayons

Activity   Draw a simple, single-line doodle on a piece of paper. Then have your child try to make this curvy pattern into some object or animal mentioned in the Bible. Take turns drawing. Talk together about the story or event that comes to mind. When you finish with the game, tell your child that you've enjoyed playing together. Say that you're happy that you two can talk about God's Word in any place and at any time. Take a moment to thank God for the fun and the love you share as parent and child.

Making Pictures

Bible Focus "Finally, brothers, whatever is true, whatever is noble, whatever is right, whatever is pure, whatever is lovely, whatever is admirable—if anything is excellent or praiseworthy—think about such things" (Phil. 4:8).

Materials paper and felt-tipped markers or crayons, Bible or Bible storybook

Activity Try one of these drawing activities: encourage your child to draw a picture about a Bible story that you've just finished reading, or listen to Christian music while drawing, or color some pictures in a Bible story coloring book and then read the story from the Bible.

Read the Bible focus verse. Tell your child that all day long, even when we're coloring, God wants us to think about things that are right and good. Pray a prayer of thanks for your special art time together.

Exploring Psalms

Bible Focus "I recite my verses for the king" (Ps. 45:1).

Materials pencil and paper

Activity Ask: "Did you know there was a hymnbook right in the middle of the Bible?" Show your child the book of Psalms while you explain that these 150 songs or poems have helped many, many people to worship God. Point out that Jesus was one who heard these psalms—the special name for the Bible's songs and poems—many times as a child.

Read a short sampling of familiar psalms—Ps. 23:1; Ps. 118:24; Ps. 100:1. Ask your child to name some words of praise found in these psalms. Or read a short section of your favorite psalm and tell why you like it. Explain the Bible focus verse: "Recite" means to say by memory; "king" means God who is our heavenly King. Help your child to recite one verse from the psalm(s) you've just read.

Then try making up your own psalm by writing down the praise sentences that relate to your family, your church, or your home. Or work together with your child to fill in the blanks and complete this one:

I will praise you in the morning, Lord.
When I *(name a morning activity)*
and when I *(name another morning activity)*
I will remember to bless your name.
At noon I will stop to give you thanks

because (*say something that God gives you*)
and because (*say a reason that you love God*).
Even when darkness comes at night,
I will still be thinking of you.
When I lie in bed I will thank you for (*name three
     things*).
Day and night, Lord,
I will remember that you are God.

Try singing your psalm. Any music you make up will
be joyful!

Exploring Proverbs

Bible Focus "He who walks with the wise grows wise" (Prov. 13:20).

Materials paper and pencil or crayons, Bible

Activity Show your child the book of Proverbs in your Bible. Explain that this book is a collection of many wise sayings that can help us to know what is right to do. Read several examples (Prov. 1:7-8 and 14:16 are good ones) including the Bible focus verse. Point out that proverbs can be easily memorized because of their shortness. Because they can be memorized, they can be helpful reminders about doing what is right.

Choose one proverb to memorize as a family or have each family member work on one proverb to recite at the dinner table. Talk about the meaning of each one, and even try rewriting some of the proverbs into simpler language so that they mean more to your young child. Continue to share proverbs until some of them become a familiar part of your family's conversation. Talk about their meanings and apply them to your own life situations.

Extra-special idea If your child enjoys drawing, have him or her make a picture about a favorite psalm or proverb. Write the verse on the finished artwork, and display it in your home or share it with a friend.

We Love Jesus!

Bible Focus "Do not be ashamed to testify about our Lord" (2 Tim. 1:8).

Materials large piece of paper or cloth and colorful paper or cloth pieces

Activity Throughout the day, make a game of looking for banners and banner-size signs in stores, schools, and other public places. Read the banners to your child. Talk about what each banner means to those who read it. Point out that banners are used to announce important messages or to tell about things in which people take pride.

Later, in your home, read the Bible focus verse. Discuss the verse in simple terms. Include talk about ways you and your child can tell others that you love Jesus (by saying grace before meals even in restaurants, inviting a neighbor to church, wearing a cross necklace, or other ideas). Then design a banner for your home that says: WE LOVE JESUS! or a banner for your child's room that says: (Child's name) LOVES JESUS! Make the banner from cloth or paper. As you work, talk about how this banner tells an important message. It's a message you can be proud of. Remind your child that actions always speak louder than words. It's how we live that really tells others whether or not we love God.

After you hang your banner, pray: Lord, it's easier to hang a banner that says we love you than to live each day showing that love. We want to act in ways that show our love for you. Use this banner to remind us that we needn't be ashamed to live for you. Amen.

Sharing with Others

Bible Focus   "And do not forget to do good and to share with others, for with such sacrifices God is pleased" (Heb. 13:16).

Materials   milk and cookies, Bible

Activity   Invite a group of children or your family to have a snack. Pour a glass of milk for each person. Then open the cookie jar. Act surprised to find a shortage of cookies. Allow the children to decide if and how cookies should be divided among the group. Help the children work toward a point of being thankful for the amount each receives. Say a prayer of thanks and/or a prayer for help to be thankful in situations where we receive less than we expect.

Point out that, when it comes to sharing, God hears what we say both out loud and in our hearts. Point out that God is ready to help us share, because God knows it is hard for us to share the things we would rather keep for ourselves. Open your Bible and read the Bible focus verse. Discuss what "sacrifices" means here. Think of other things—besides today's cookies—that God might be wanting you to share.

Talk about how "sacrificing" for someone else might be a good way to show that you really care about that person. Ask each child and parent to think about something he or she would be willing to do or share to help a person in need. Make plans to carry out at least one "sharing project" within the week.

Pray and thank God for giving us things to share and for understanding when it is difficult for us to share.

Rainbows and Promises

Bible Focus "The LORD is faithful to all his promises and loving toward all he has made" (Ps. 145:13).

Materials water color paints and paper or food coloring, water, eyedroppers, and white paper plates

Activity Begin with a discussion about promises: What is a promise? What are some promises that we have made to each other? Point out the relationship between promises and trust: If we want people to trust us, we must be careful to keep the promises we make. (Don't shy away from talking about broken promises that have affected your family. Be ready to give and ask for forgiveness.)

Read the Bible focus verse. Ask your child if we can trust God. (*Yes, because God always keeps promises. When the Bible says God is faithful, that's another way of saying that God always keeps promises.*) List some of God's promises—God will always be with us; God will give eternal life to those who believe in Jesus.

In your own words, tell the story of the promise God gave when he put the rainbow in the sky (Gen. 9:12-16). Invite your child to paint colorful rainbows as you tell the story. (Show older preschoolers how the rainbow colors can be made by blending the primary colors—yellow, red, and blue, or have them stack the colors as they appear in the sky—red, orange, yellow, green, blue, indigo, and violet.) Display the rainbows as reminders that God keeps promises and that we should keep ours, too.

Instead of making pictures, you may try this activity: Make small jars of the three primary colors—red, blue, yellow—by mixing water with several drops of food coloring. Let your child experiment with making new colors by mixing drops of colored water together on a white paper plate. If you dampen the plate first, the colors will fuse together.

Extra-special idea On a hot, sunny day, do the "Promises and Rainbows" activity by making rainbow colors appear in the fine mist spray from a garden hose.

Forty Days

Bible Focus "For forty days the flood kept coming on the earth" (Gen. 7:17).

Materials a calendar and a rainy day or a day when it's hard to wait for something to happen

Activity Talk about waiting: "Waiting is hard, isn't it? When I have trouble waiting, I think about Noah inside the ark. Do you know how many days it rained while he and his family waited inside?" (*Forty.*) Take a calendar and count back 40 days. Pick an event that your child can remember that happened about 40 days ago or count ahead 40 days to see what you might be doing. Use these dates to help your child understand the length of 40 days. Say: "Forty days is a long time! But do you know that Noah had to wait even longer— weeks longer—before he and his family and the animals could go outside again? That was a long, long time to wait!"

Talk about how when waiting gets hard, we can remember that God wants to be in control of time. We can talk to God about waiting. We can ask God to take charge of each minute of our lives. We can ask God to help us to be patient, even as Noah was patient. Pray, asking God for patience, and saying thanks for the good plan God has for each day of our lives.

Looking for Cornerstones

Bible Focus   "Christ Jesus himself [is] the chief cornerstone" (Eph. 2:20).

Setting   a short car trip or a walking tour

Activity   Explore a section of your town or city, looking for cornerstones. (Cornerstones are often found on public buildings.) Conclude your search by looking for the cornerstone of your own church building. Talk about the importance of cornerstones: Every other part of the building is placed on top of the cornerstone and if the cornerstone is not straight and strong, the walls might be crooked or weak. The cornerstone also often tells the date on which the building was finished or other important information. Sometimes cornerstones are hollow so that they can hold information about the people who built the building.

As you stand in front of your church cornerstone, read the Bible focus verse. Ask why Jesus is called the chief (main) cornerstone. Have your child touch the church made of bricks and mortar. Then take your child's hand. Explain that God is building a church that is not made with bricks or wood. God is building a church that is made with people. Jesus is the perfect, strong cornerstone of this church. All the rest of us who believe in him are like "living stones" (1 Peter 2:5) in this church. We join with Jesus to make a church that can love others and do God's work. The "living church" of which we are a part is so big and so widespread that we can see only a little bit of it. It goes from the beginning to the end of history, and it is spread throughout the whole world.

Hold hands and say this scripture verse: "In (Jesus) the whole building is joined together and rises to become a holy temple in the Lord. And in (Jesus) you too are being built together to become a dwelling in which God lives by his Spirit" (Eph. 2:21-22). While you're still holding hands, pray: *Thank you, God, for building your church with living stones like* (name special church friends and family). *Amen.*

Sweeter Than Honey

Bible Focus "[God's rules] are sweeter than honey, than honey from the comb" (Ps. 19:10).

Materials honey, especially a piece of honeycomb, and bread

Activity Share a snack of bread and honey. As you eat, talk about David's words in Psalm 19: David wrote a song that said that God's ways (God's rules) are sweeter than honey. Ask how honey tastes. David loved God, and he thought God's rules were good. Following God's ways made David happy.

Explain to your child how following God's ways has brought blessings in your life. Talk about what God wants us to do. Let your child add his or her own ideas.

Maybe you like sugar or syrup better than honey, but even so, keep the honey jar on the table for several days as a reminder that God's ways (God's rules) are good. Repeat the Bible focus verse during mealtime. Say grace before each meal.

Extra-special food ideas Foods can prod us to think about many Bible-related topics. Here's some "food for thought":

■ What did people eat in Bible times? Start a list by reading these passages to your child: 2 Sam. 17:29; Prov. 27:18; Luke 9:13. Add to your list as you come upon more foods during personal quiet times or family devotions. Look through a Bible dictionary or other reference book to learn more about foods in Jesus' time. Try lentils, olives, figs, or other foods listed.

■ Why do we say grace before meals? Let children give their own answers to this question. Explain Jesus' teaching in Matt. 6:31-33 in your own words. Thank God for giving food. Try saying grace after a meal using the Bible focus scripture in Deut. 8:10: "When you have eaten and are satisfied, praise the Lord your God. . . ."

■ Have an outdoor fish fry. Then around the campfire tell your children the story of Jesus' cooking fish for his friends (John 21:9 and surrounding verses).

■ Bake bread together or choose a special loaf from the grocer's shelf. Talk about how important bread is to our physical lives. Read some of the many scripture verses about bread: Deut. 8:3; Matt. 6:11; etc. Share your bread with neighbors or friends.

Traveling without Maps

Bible Focus "[The Lord] gently leads those that have young" (Isa. 40:11).

Materials map for a trip, Bible

Activity Plan a trip by looking at a map. Point out your hometown and the place you will visit. Help your child to trace the best route to the destination. Ask: "Do you know why we need a map for this trip? What would it be like to travel without one?"

Then talk about Bible people who traveled without maps. Read about Abram's journey in Gen. 12:1. God didn't give Abram a map. God showed him the way. God also led Moses on a long journey. Read Exod. 13:21. In both stories God gave the people special "guidance."

Say: "As Christians, we believe that God still gives us guidance. We don't have paper maps that tell us where God wants us to live, where Daddy or Mommy should work, where you should go to school. But we believe God will guide us as we pray and study the Bible. In a way, our lives are like Abram's and Moses's lives; we have to make many important decisions that aren't written out on paper maps. But we can trust God for guidance when we have no map." Read the Bible focus verse, and pray a prayer of thanks for guidance.

Clothes

Bible Focus "He has clothed me with garments of salvation" (Isa. 61:10).

Materials wedding photographs

Activity Look at the photographs and talk about why the bride and groom are dressed so beautifully.

Read the Bible focus verse, including all of verse 10. Talk with your child about the Bible words: "Sometimes the Bible uses things we can see to help us understand things we can't see. Like the clothes the bride and groom are wearing in the picture, the clothes we just read about are beautiful. But the Bible is talking about something that we can't see with our eyes. When we become Christians God changes us inside. It's as though God takes off our old ugly sinfulness and puts on new clothes of salvation. Salvation makes us look beautiful to God. Do you want to know what we look like inside before God saves us?" Read Isa. 64:6: ". . . all our righteous acts are like filthy (dirty) rags." Talk about the difference between rags and beautiful clothes. Ask: "When God looks inside our hearts what do you think God sees?" Tell your child that God forgives our sins. God loves us even when we are not beautiful on the inside.

Pray and ask God to dress you in beautiful "spiritual" clothes by the power of the Holy Spirit.

Extra-special clothes ideas A preschooler spends many hours learning how to get dressed. Use these ideas while your preschooler is dressing.

■ Talk about Dorcas as you sew or mend your child's clothes. Then read about her in Acts 9:36-42. Talk about how much she meant to the Christians in Joppa because of the work she did for others. Thank God that even simple jobs like mending can be important ways to serve others in the church.

■ Talk about Samuel's new coats as you try on clothes from last year. Point out that many of the clothes which fit last year are too small this year. When you're done sorting clothes in your child's closet, take time to talk about Samuel and his mother Hannah (1 Samuel 1-4). Tell how his mother had to make him a new coat every year. Talk about the blessing she had in seeing her son grow up to serve the Lord. Pray together, asking that your child will continue to grow in the knowledge of God.

■ Talk about Joseph's special coat when your child gets new clothes (Genesis 37). Point out that Joseph's coat was a sign of his father's love, but that it also caused jealousy among his brothers. Talk about your child's new clothes. Do they make him or her feel more important than others? Do they cause jealousy? Is the child jealous when someone else gets something that he or she doesn't have? Then point out that Joseph was important not because of what he wore, but because he believed firmly in God. His brothers took his coat away, but they could not take his trust in God away.

It's What's Inside That Counts

Bible Focus "I will strengthen you" (Isa. 41:10).

Materials prepackaged foods

Activity Find out what is in the foods you eat by reading the ingredients to your child. Help your child to decide which ingredients strengthen the body and which are bad. Take your child grocery shopping or plan a meal together so that healthful foods are emphasized.

Read the Bible focus verse. Tell your child that God is not just interested in strengthening (or making stronger) our physical bodies. God wants to strengthen our faith and our love for Christ, too. Talk about some good spiritual ingredients for a strong faith life (*prayer, devotions, thoughtful acts to others, etc.*). After having a healthful meal for your body, have a "healthful" devotion to strengthen your faith. Then thank God in prayer for the things that strengthen your body and your faith.

What Was It Like When . . . ?

Bible Focus   "Jesus Christ is the same yesterday, today and forever" (Heb. 13:8).

Materials   old family photographs

Activity   Capitalize on your child's curiosity about what it was like when you were young. Tour your house, pointing out the differences between your present kitchen and your mother's kitchen, your child's games and your own childhood games, etc. Use old pictures to show the kind of car you rode in, the style you wore your hair, or other interesting facets of your childhood. Invite grandparents to play this game, too. Let them tell what life was like when they were young.

Discuss how even though styles and fashions change, needs stay the same. Point out that food, water, and protection are needs that all people—past and present—have. In addition, explain that people also have an unchanging spiritual need for a Savior to rescue them from sin. Jesus is that Savior.

Read the Bible focus verse and ask: "Is Jesus someone who changes or someone who is always the same? (The same.) When he died on the cross, he died for your sins, and Mommy's and Daddy's sins, and Grandpa's and Grandma's sins. He is the Savior of people who lived long ago, of those who live right now, and of those who will be born in the future.

Pray together, thanking God for sending a Savior to people of all places and times.

You Asked for It

Bible Focus   "Which of you, if his son asks for bread, will give him a stone?" (Matt. 7:9).

Materials   stone, peanut butter or jelly, Bible

Activity   Wait for a time when your child asks you for a piece of bread with jelly or peanut butter on it. Promptly comply with the request by spreading jelly or peanut butter onto a large, clean stone. Wait for your child's reaction, and then talk about why he or she was so surprised to get a stone instead of bread. Make your child an edible snack, and then read the Bible focus verse. Tell your child that Jesus used this very story to teach people more about what God is like.

Reread the Bible focus verse, and add verses 10 and 11. Say that even though you try to be a good parent when choosing what is right to give your child, there are times when you might give the wrong thing. Say that God never gives us the wrong things when we ask. God always gives us what we really need. Ask: "Are you willing to trust God when you pray? Does God always hear? Does God always understand what we need?" (*God always hears and understands. God even understands our need better than we do, and God answers prayer—though not always with the answer we look for.*) Have your child offer one thing about which to pray. Then you share one of your prayer concerns. Together pray about these two needs. Close your time together by praying: *Thank you, Lord, that you know our needs. You are a good heavenly Father who gives good things to his children. Amen.*

Jesus Can Do Anything

Bible Focus   "For I have come down from heaven not to do my will but to do the will of him who sent me" (John 6:38).

Materials   stones

Activity   A young child's first religious queries sometimes center on Jesus' or God's capabilities. A child will glibly say, "God can do anything, can't he? Even turn our dog blue—if he wants to."

When such conversations come your way, direct your child's thinking to the true nature of God: God does powerful things. But in addition to being all powerful, God is also perfect and all wise. God's actions always show power, wisdom, and perfection wrapped up together. God does not use power just to thrill or entertain us.

Place some stones in front of your child, and ask whether Jesus could turn these stones into bread. Answer the question by reading how the devil tempted Christ (Matt. 4:1-3). Talk about these things: Did hungry Jesus turn the stones to bread? *(Matt. 4:4.)* Could he have? *(Yes.)* Then why didn't he? *(Because he knew it was not God's will.)* Read the rest of the story (Matt. 4:5-11). Talk about how Jesus never used power in a wrong way. He did not give in to the devil's tests.

In the same way, we don't expect to see God's power for thrills or entertainment. We do believe God's power can bring about God's will. Review the Bible focus verse and pray: *Thank you, God, that you are all powerful, perfect, and all wise. Amen.*

Molds

Bible Focus   "Don't let the world squeeze you into its mold" (Rom. 12:2 Phillips).

Materials   clay and a collection of plastic, metal, and natural molds

Activity   Read the Bible focus verse and talk about its meaning: God does not want us to copy the world's way of living; we are to follow Jesus. We can let other people mold our thinking, or we can let Gold mold our thinking. Hand out some clay, and explain that you are going to find out what it means to have something squeezed into a mold. Show your child how to use simple molds such as bottle tops, acorn caps, doll dishes, etc. Then experiment by pressing the clay into molds. Point out that the clay always takes on the shape of the mold. After you've played for a while, talk about the Bible focus verse again. Ask: "Do we ever copy other people's actions? When we do, aren't we a little like clay that copies whatever shape it is pressed against? Other people's thoughts and actions can be like molds. When we start letting our own thoughts and actions get squeezed to be the same as theirs, we start thinking and acting as they do. Sometimes this can cause problems, if their thinking is not right. As people who love Christ, who are we supposed to be copying? (Jesus.) That's why the Bible tells us to be careful; it's easy to copy someone else and get squeezed into doing something that does not please God."

Talk about specific temptations and struggles that you and your child face. Then pray: *Dear Jesus, we want to think and act in ways that please you. Forgive us for the times when we copy people whose thoughts and actions do not please you. Amen.*

Extra-special activity with clay Talk about the things that a potter can make with clay. Encourage your child to pretend to be a potter and make something with the clay. Then share the words of Isa. 64:8: "We are the clay; you (God) are the potter; we are all the work of your hand." Rejoice in the fact that God is a perfect potter. Assure your child that God doesn't make mistakes. God has made you just as God wanted you to be, according to God's own design. When your child struggles with self-acceptance, remind him or her of this verse.

Looking for Light

Bible Focus "The people walking in darkness have seen a great light" (Isa. 9:2).

Materials flashlight

Activity This is best done in the evening, or in a room that can be darkened. Before you begin the activity, hide a lighted flashlight in one of the rooms of your house. Then meet with your child in another room, and read the Bible focus verse. Ask what it is like to walk in darkness. Let your child list some of the problems. Then turn out all the lights and try walking in darkness. Head toward the room that has the flashlight.

Talk about how you found the light in the darkness. Then say that when the Bible talks about "walking in darkness" it doesn't just mean the kind of darkness you were walking in. This verse is talking about spiritual darkness. Spiritual darkness means living without God.

Explain that hate, anger, and selfishness are some of the things people experience when they choose to live without God. When Jesus came, he said to the people "I am the light of the world" (John 8:12). Tell your child that God has given us two kinds of light—the light we can know with our eyes and the light we can know with our hearts. If we want to get rid of the darkness in our house, what can we do? (Turn on the lights.) How do we get rid of the darkness of hate, anger, or meanness inside our hearts? An electric light bulb can't take care of that kind of darkness. But Jesus can come inside our lives and bring the light of his love. Give your child a hug and pray: Jesus, we want the light of your love to be in our hearts. Amen.

Unknown Ways

Bible Focus "And if I go and prepare a place for you, I will come back and take you to be with me" (John 14:3).

Materials a stamped and addressed letter to put in the mail

Activity When your child asks "Where is heaven?" or "How does someone go to heaven?" say that we don't know the full answers to these questions. At the same time assure your child that Jesus knows where heaven is and how to take us there. Read your child the Bible focus verse about heaven, and then do this activity to help explain its meaning.

Write a letter to a friend in another town. Have your child include whatever doodles and writings he or she chooses. Then say that you are closing the letter with the following message: Dear *(friend's name):* Please write or call me when this letter gets to your house. Mommy (Daddy) will have a special talk with me about heaven on the day we hear that you got my note. Thank you. Love, *(child's name).*

Send the letter and wait for a reply. When you hear from your friend, spend some time talking about the letter and how it got to your friend's house. Then ask: "Did we have to know *how* the postal service worked in order for the letter to get there safely? No, we only needed to trust the mail carrier enough to give him (her) the letter. The post office did the rest. Our mail gets safely to our friends' homes even though we don't know exactly how it travels there."

Explain that mailing a letter can help us understand about how someone gets to heaven. Read the Bible focus verse and talk about Jesus' promise. He has gone to heaven to prepare a place for us. He will come to take us there himself. We do not need to know where heaven is or how to get there. We only need to know that heaven is where Jesus is. And we trust Jesus' promise that we will be with him in heaven. He can take us to heaven even better than a mail carrier can get a letter to another town.

Thank Jesus for preparing a place for us and for coming for us when it's time to go to heaven.

Freed from Sin

4-5

Bible Focus   "[Jesus] . . . has freed us from our sins" (Rev. 1:5).

Materials   masking tape, Bible

Activity   Have your child tape your fingers and thumb together. Try to turn the pages of the Bible or do other simple tasks.

Then have your child free your fingers by removing the tape. Tape your child's hand and let the child experiment as you did. Talk about what it's like to have a hand "bound" with tape and a hand "freed" from tape. Which hand can do more things? Which hand is easier to use?

Read the Bible focus verse. Point out the word *freed*. Explain how you were freed from sin to live for God when you believed that Christ died to save you from your sins. Talk about a true story that shows how being freed from sin by believing in Jesus' death and resurrection made it easier to do the right thing for another person. Encourage your child to talk about his or her own thoughts on Jesus' death and resurrection.

Pray: *Thank you, Jesus, that you died to free me from sin. Amen.*

4-5

Learning to Accept Change

Bible Focus   "When you sow, you do not plant the body that will be, but just a seed" (1 Cor. 15:37).

Materials   pretty packets of seeds and soil to plant them in

Activity   Pick out a variety of pretty flowers that will grow in your area. Show the picture on the packet to your child. Talk about how beautiful the flowers are. Then look inside.

Ask: "Are seeds as pretty as the flowers?" Talk about how each kind of flower grows from its own kind of seed. Plant the seeds according to directions. Then point out that the seed is going to have to change in order for the flowers to grow. Gardeners have to give up their seeds if they want to be able to hope for flowers. Read the Bible focus verse. Explain that it will take time for the flowers to grow.

As days go by, watch for green shoots. When you see them, again talk about the changes taking place. The seed has changed—it has "died" or disappeared—in order for the plant to grow. Ask whether the child would rather have the seed or the plant. Continue to monitor the growth of your plants as they mature and bloom. Then compare the flower's beauty with the seed's.

Use this gardening experience to talk about changes that come about when you have to move or when someone you know dies, etc. Facing change usually is hard for both children and parents, but change can be for the better. If a seed never changed, it could never grow a flower. If you never changed homes, you might lose the opportunity to meet new friends. If people never died, no one could look forward to trading pain and illness for the wonderful experience of being alive with Christ in heaven.

Be sensitive to your child's reluctance to accept change. When the time for change comes, encourage your child to be open about his or her feelings. When you are considering changes, allow your child to be a prayer-partner in asking for God's guidance. Help your child to express needs to God as he or she anticipates change and goes through change.

Through the Glass

Bible Focus   "For now we see through a glass, darkly; but then face to face" (1 Cor. 13:12 KJV).

Materials   child's sunglasses, petroleum jelly

Activity   Rub petroleum jelly on the lenses of the sunglasses. Then have your child put on the glasses and tell you what different things in the room look like. Give your child plenty of time to explore. Take off the glasses. Ask "Do things look different now? Why?"

Read the Bible focus verse and offer an explanation: "It says that now we see through a glass darkly; then we will see things face to face. Do you hear the two different times that are mentioned—now and then? When I can't understand how God is working, I think about this verse. Right *now*, I can't see exactly what God is like—it's like looking through these glasses that stop me from seeing things as they really are. But *then*— and the then means when I finally see God face to face— I will understand everything because the glasses that make things unclear will be gone.

"Some people say that they don't want to believe in God because they can't understand the way God does things. But here the Bible explains that we won't be able to understand everything clearly right now. When we see God face to face we will understand.

Talk about your child's thoughts. Then pray: *Lord, we know we don't have to understand you completely right now to love you and trust you. Thank you, God, that someday we will see you face to face. Amen.*

3

Special Days with God
Devotions for Holidays

I am collecting memories for our family museum!
—Edith Schaeffer, *What Is A Family?*

What a holiday we would have if our favorite singer or writer or artist came to spend the day with us! Then why are we so casual about giving a place of honor to Jesus—the King of kings—on holidays, even on those that commemorate his birth or resurrection? As Christian parents we must fight the trends that turn our holidays into hollow-days. The traditions we establish in our homes and the memories we make with them will be with our children for a lifetime.

Seasonal devotional materials, magazine features, and books on creating holiday memories can direct you to ideas that are right for your family. (See the "References and Further Reading" list on page 141 for suggestions.) Start a file of good ideas. Some of the devotional activities in Chapter 2 are also well-suited for holiday use. Here is a sampling of what can be done to keep your focus on Christ during important holidays.

Christmas

■ Count down the days. Observing the season of Advent, the four weeks preceding Christmas, is a good way to anticipate Christmas. Check your child's Sunday school take-home papers. Often some type of calendar or activity is included to mark off the days to Christmas. Or purchase an Advent calendar with scripture readings and/or activities that your child can use daily. You can turn an ordinary calendar into an Advent calendar by planning your own schedule of devotions and activities. Mark in all your responsibilities (such as caroling at the retirement home, shopping for family gifts, or sending cards) as a way of lessening last-minute pressures. Schedule family time for play and relaxation, too.

■ Enjoy an Advent wreath. Make the construction of an Advent wreath from greens and four candles an annual family project. Each Sunday in Advent, set aside a special devotional time that ends with the lighting of the appropriate candles. Adapt the following activities from Chapter 2 for use during the four Sundays of Advent:

First Sunday—"Looking for Light" (page 88). On the first night of Advent hide the family Advent wreath along with the lighted flashlight. Have the whole family search while the house is totally dark. When the wreath is found, put it in a prominent place (such as your dining table). Talk about the Bible focus verse and how these words were written many years before Christ's birth. Explain what *prophecy* means, and then light the first candle, the "Prophecy Candle." Pray and thank God that you know Jesus Christ.

Second Sunday—"Names" (page 56). On the second Sunday, light the Prophecy Candle, and review what you talked about the week before. Then do the "Names" activity to find out how Jesus got his name. Talk about the other preparations that Mary made for Jesus and that you made for your child's birth. Then light the second candle, the "Bethlehem Candle" as a reminder of the place that was prepared for Christ's coming. Pray and ask that your own hearts will have room for Christ.

Third Sunday—"First Baby Stories" (page 54). On the third Sunday, light the two candles from the previous weeks. Review their names and stories. Do the "First Baby Stories" activity. Include mention of the shepherds' visit. Then light the third candle, the "Shepherds' Candle." Pray and thank God that the good news about Jesus keeps on being told.

Fourth Sunday—"The Family Gift Box" (page 55). On the fourth Sunday, light the three candles and review your Advent celebration to date. Then talk about love as being the most important part of Christmas. It was God's love that sent Jesus. It should be love that makes us want to share gifts and have a good holiday. Talk about how selfishness instead of love often sets in right before Christmas. Use "The Family Gift Box" as a way of directing attention back to others' needs and the true meaning of love. Light the fourth candle, the "Angels' Candle" and thank God for sending Jesus from heaven to earth to show us real love.

Christmas Day—"Happy Birthday, Jesus." As you light all the candles on your wreath on Christmas day, sing "Happy Birthday, Jesus." Let your child share what has made this Christmas special.

■ Gather around the tree. The soft light of the Christmas tree is conducive to family quiet times. Make scrolls to hang on your tree by writing down favorite family verses or scriptures saved from your child's take-home Sunday school papers. Roll them up, and tie with a piece of yarn. For devotions have your child choose a scroll and talk about the scripture. Or hang activity ideas such as "lead a prayer," or "sing a song" on your tree, and use them as devotion-starters during the Christmas season. You can even use your tree for a series of object lessons by talking about branches (John 15:5), roots (Isa. 11:10), soil (Matt. 13:24), lights (Gen. 1:3), star (Matt. 2:2), and tree (Ps. 1:3). In each case, show that the tree can remind us of an important truth about our relationship with God.

■ Who is this Santa Claus? As a family with one or more preschoolers, you must decide what to say about Santa. We have found that our celebration of Christ's birth has more than enough true wonders to captivate our hearts and imaginations. We talk of real angels, real shepherds, and real kings as we relate the events of Jesus' birth. We don't risk watering down these true historic visits with an added mixture of stories about a Santa Claus who comes down chimneys. Our children know that, at best, Santa Claus stories came from stories about a Christian man who gave gifts to poor people a long time ago. We have fun playing "Santa" ourselves as we find ways to share with others. The seasonal songs and poetry about Santa Claus can be used to start conversations about people who are happy to give gifts to others.

Easter

■ Celebrate new life. "What does a bunny have to do with Easter?" our five-year-old asked. Bunnies, chicks, flowers, and eggs can be symbols of new life. All these traditional Easter trappings, however, fall short of describing the new life of Christ's resurrection. Prepare your child for Easter by talking about Jesus' trial and death on a cross. A three-year-old can understand that Jesus died, even though he or she can't completely comprehend why. The young child can sense the sadness of that event and can contrast that sadness with the happy news that Jesus came to life again on Easter.

As a special activity, prepare an Easter basket with hollow plastic eggs. Put a symbol of new life (a baby bunny, a tiny egg, a flower, etc.) in each one. Have your child open each egg, and talk about how each thing inside reminds us of the new life that we see in spring. Then have your preschooler open an egg with nothing inside. Tell your child that *empty* is one of Easter's most important words. Use the egg to show what empty means. Talk about the *empty* tomb, and how it proved that Jesus really rose from the dead.* Read a simple retelling of the resurrection story. Then pray with your child.

Halloween

Those who work with children will tell you that next to Christmas, children like Halloween best. Because of its dubious spiritual roots and the dangers of going from house to house by night, however, many Christians see the need to divert their childrens' attention from this celebration. Fun alternatives to this holiday can include activities related to harvest time and All Saints' Day (November 1).

*This activity was adapted from the story "Jeremiah's Easter" by Ida Mae Kempel as published in *Focus on the Family,* April 1988, pp. 2-3.

■ Give treats instead of tricks. Make a homemade costume with your child that does not conjure up thoughts of horror and evil. Instead of trick-or-treating on the designated night, stay home to answer the door. Make a special treat that can be both eaten and given away. Then during the daylight hours on All Saints' Day, have your child dress up and deliver special treats to your neighbors. (Our experience has shown that neighbors like getting instead of giving, and our preschoolers still get to show off their outfits to neighborhood friends.) Center your quiet time that day on being a cheerful giver or on the life of a saint who showed Christ's way to others.

■ Expand these wholesome activities into church-wide events—have a "Dress Up Like a Saint Party," a harvest party, or a "Let's Go Treating" activity to a nearby hospital or care facility. Make corporate worship a short and active part of these fun events.

Thanksgiving

Outside of the big meal and the visits of friends and relatives, preschoolers have little to look forward to on this holiday. Still, a national holiday for giving thanks should not be taken lightly, especially by Christian families. You can spice up Thanksgiving by establishing meaningful traditions and doing fun activities.

■ Give thanks. If you're traveling, try some versions of the "The Gratefulness Game" (page 39). For a real challenge, make a clock face with movable hands and write some things that you are thankful for beside each hour of the day. Then see if you and your child can remember to stop and pray a prayer of thanks during each hour of Thanksgiving Day. Move the clock hands to show that you have prayed. Or plan a special prayer of thanks using some of the ideas from Chapter 6: Special Ways to Pray.

■ Review the past. Read a story about the Plymouth Plantation. Define the word *pilgrim*. Make special pilgrim hats or Indian headbands to wear at the dinner table. Or have an activity on food by eating something that is traditionally associated with the first thanksgiving feast. In the evening, prepare a cold supper without using modern kitchen conveniences. Eat by candlelight. Talk about the hardships endured by those who came to the New World to find freedom of worship.

Birthdays

What better time to say "You're special to God and me" than on your child's birthday? At bedtime or in your quiet time during the day, have a one-to-one talk with your child. Hug your child. Tell your child how special he or she is. Point out where the Bible says that we are "fearfully and wonderfully made" (Ps. 139:14). Listen to any special joys or fears your child has about getting older. Then gently place your hands on your child's head and pray for your child as he or she begins a new year.

Other Special Days

Even a young child's life can be punctuated by events that are unusually happy or sad. New questions arise when the child encounters circumstances for the first time. A preschooler needs quiet moments in which to talk about feelings and questions when they come.

Prayer and forethought on what to say when your child asks questions about hard subjects like death can prepare you to be a good listener and a comforting support. Here are some situations that merit special quiet times:

Today I saw someone baptized. Though preschoolers may not be able to understand all that takes place at baptism, they can comprehend certain aspects. Water and washing are familiar to the youngest children. You can help them understand baptism by telling them that it is a washing away of sin. Talk about Jesus' baptism (Matt. 3:13-17), the beginning of Paul's walk with Jesus (Acts 9:18), and the baptism of a jailer and his family (Acts 16:31-34). Explain that in every part of the world Christians baptize those who become part of the church. We have been commanded by Jesus to "go and make disciples . . . baptizing them in the name of the Father and of the Son and of the Holy Spirit" (Matt. 28:19). Like the jailer, we are happy when someone is baptized.

Today I saw someone take communion. As with baptism, a preschooler is too young to understand the abstract concepts involving communion. Answering questions about the bread and the cup can start with a short look at Jesus and his disciples during the Last Supper (Luke 22:7-19). Point out how Jesus shared bread and passed the cup during his last meal with his disciples before he died on the cross. Talk about Paul's words in 1 Cor. 11:26: "For whenever you eat this bread and drink this cup, you proclaim the Lord's death until he comes." As Christians take communion, they remember that Jesus died on the cross for their sins. They remember that he rose from the death and that he will be coming again.

Today someone I know died. It is perhaps easier to give quick answers to a young child who is touched by death than to let that child work through puzzlement and grief in his or her own way. When death is distant and holds little or no sadness for the child, your talks can center on what death is, on heaven, and on how death is a part of living. The activities "Through the Glass" (page 94) and "Learning to Accept Change" (page 92) and "Unknown Ways" (page 89) can be used to talk about the death of an acquaintance or stranger. When a loved one dies, however, these discussions probably will be inadequate. A preschooler needs time to develop an understanding that death is permanent. You must be a good listener to help the child understand his or her fear, anger, and sadness. Look for helpful books and competent Christian support to help a young child through the loss of a close relative or friend.

Children also grieve for animals and pets that die. Don't push aside grief, even if it's for a dead caterpillar. It might comfort your child to know that not one sparrow falls to the ground without God's knowledge (Matt. 10:29); that God loves all creatures so much that God personally spent time with Adam while the animals were being named (Gen. 2:19); and that nature itself looks forward to the day when death and sadness will end (Rom. 8:22-23). Jesus understands our sadness and our love for animals. He can help us even when we feel sad.

4

Storytime with God

Devotions Using Books for Children

A good book is the best of friends . . .
—Martin F. Tupper

We make the world accessible to our children when we offer them books. What's more, as we read to our children, we travel with them on their first literary adventures; we point the way, stop by the places that were dear to us as children, and prepare our little ones for further explorations that can last a lifetime. When we read together, we talk together, we share together, we think together. And though the things we share and think about spring from the book in our hands, we are not confined by its printed pages. Each reading experience gives us an opportunity to explore life, and each opportunity to explore life gives us an opportunity to look for God.

The following activities include specific ways to make books and other reading materials a meaningful part of family devotions. A list of helpful books and magazines is included in the References and Further Reading section on page 141.

Reading Activities with Preschoolers

From your child's infancy: Build some of your child's quiet times around books. Read your own daily devotions out loud. Include the reading of prayers, poetry, and hymns while you cuddle your baby. Make the most of these tender times of sharing, because they won't last long. At six months your child probably will be responding to bright pictures in your reading material. By eight months your little partner already may be too active for this sort of quiet time. When little hands want to turn the pages you're reading and a little mouth makes literal attempts to devour the scriptures, it's time to add new reading activities!

From one to two years: When your child reaches out for your books, create a "library" for your preschooler. Provide both durable books made from cardboard or cloth and regular books that have realistic, colorful illustrations. Practice "active" reading: point to familiar objects, ask simple recognition questions, and emphasize expression, rhythm, and rhyme.

From three to five years: Continue to add new ways to make reading fun. Combine library trips with a stop for ice cream or a supper out. Become familiar with good children's books and make your reading count. Help your child to make good selections. Endure the "favorites" that must be read at least two dozen times.

Find out how teachers and librarians encourage reading. Help your church and circle of friends to establish similar activities that will encourage the use of Christ-centered literature. Even before your child can read, give your preschooler a Bible to treasure and to take to Sunday school. A love for God's Word and an appreciation for reading are things that can be modeled, so keep your own Bible and good books handy.

Choosing and Using Bible Storybooks

Pick a Bible storybook that is well-designed for your child. Look for one with an abundance of pictures. The best books for preschoolers have an illustration for every story. The pictures should be realistic, colorful, and full of interesting details. Each picture should fall with the text so that the child can view it while you read. If the book uses discussion questions, see if they are appropriate for your child's age level. Once you've picked out several good possibilities, it can be fun to let your child make the final selection.

In addition to providing daily reading, your child's Bible stories book can be used for a variety of learning activities:

■ Colors. Page through the book and look for certain colors. Talk about the colors in one picture as part of your discussion.

■ Counting. Use counting as a way to increase your child's interest in the stories and illustrations: How many camels do you see? How many women are listening to Jesus in this picture?

■ Alphabet Hunt. Look back over a paragraph of the story you have just finished. Look for certain letters in the text. Go on an "H" hunt or a "T" hunt, etc.

■ Relationships. Use the stories and pictures to talk about relationships: Where is this boy's father? Which girl is taller? Which fish is longer?

■ Time Sequence. Read several stories in sequence, and then talk about time: Here Samuel is a young boy listening to God in the night, and here he is, many years later, serving God as an old man. As a review, talk about the stories you've read: Which story comes first in the Bible, the story about Noah or Moses?

■ Faces. Take a close look at people's faces in a certain illustration. What emotions do they show? Why? How would you feel if you were there? Show me that expression on your face.

Ways to Share Books and Magazines

Talk with others in your community and church about your child's interest in reading, and find ways to facilitate the sharing of good books and magazines.

Familiarize yourself and your child with the materials in your local public library. Read good books and use them as springboards for talks about God and how God wants to have a personal relationship with us: When the book's hero comes to a difficult choice does he or she pray? What would you pray to God if you had to make this choice? This person is unhappy. Would you be her friend?

Get to know your children's books. Increase awareness of your church's library books by working with Sunday school teachers or vacation Bible school leaders to have a special "read-in." Set a certain time limit and let families read as many books together as possible within that time. Have sponsors who will contribute money according to the numbers of books read. Then use this money to buy new books. Sign out books from the church library for use in your daily quiet times.

Start a church-sponsored weekly storytime for preschoolers in your congregation or neighborhood. Have occasional puppet shows, author's visits, field trips, and refreshment times to supplement the regular offering. Include some songs and a time of prayer so the children can have a fun time of worship and learning.

My Own Bible

Bible Focus   "All Scripture is God-breathed . . ."
(2 Tim. 3:16).

Materials   your Bible and a Bible to give to your child

Activity   Begin this devotional period by presenting your child with a Bible. Also bring the Bible you use for devotions and worship. Ask: "Have you ever thought about how wonderful it is to have the Word of God written down for us so that we can read it day by day?"

If your child is four or five, help to find the Bible focus verse by pointing out its location in the New Testament and by pointing out the number 2 for second and the letter T starting Timothy. Read the verse. Talk about the word *inspiration:* "It's a big word that can mean 'God-breathed.' " Hold out your hand to feel your own breath as you talk. Then leaf through the Bible, from Genesis to Revelation, and talk about this wonderful story of God's love for humankind. Explain that God used special persons to write it down.

Talk about Timothy. Read 2 Tim. 3:14-17 and tell his story in your own words: He began learning about God's inspired Scriptures when he was very young. What Bible stories do you think he knew when he was three years old (or your child's age)? (*Mention some familiar Old Testament ones.*) When Timothy grew up he was a strong man of God. Formally present the Bible to your child, saying: "This is your Bible. I want you to take good care of it and use it wisely because the Bible is very important to us."

Invite your child to pray: *Heavenly Father, hear my prayer. May your holy Word make* (child's name) *"wise for salvation through faith in Christ Jesus" just as it did for Timothy. Amen.*

Encourage your child to pray for you: *Dear God, help my* (Mommy/Daddy) *to know the Bible. Amen.*

Extra-special idea Sometimes choose to use your child's Bible for family devotions.

My Favorite Bible Story Book

Bible Focus "[The king] is to read [the law] all the days of his life so that he may learn to revere the Lord his God" (Deut. 17:19).

Materials A Bible storybook

Activity Read the Bible focus verse and explain that this was one of the rules for having a good king in the promised land. God knew that a person who loved God's words and read them every day would grow to love God. We believe this still is true, and that is why we try to read the Bible every day.

Show your child the Bible storybook, and say: "Here is a Bible storybook that we can read together. Let's see if we can read it every day. If I forget, you remind me. If we go on a trip, we'll take this book along. Let's start making the reading of God's Word very important in our family. Let's learn what God has to say."

Read the first story. Talk about it while you read or after you read. Pray a short closing prayer thanking God for the Bible and God's love for you.

Our Family Story

Bible Focus   "[God] who began a good work in you will carry it on to completion" (Phil. 1:6).

Materials   family photos and a scrapbook

Activity   Work together to make a family scrapbook. If your child seems too eager to offer help, give him or her a separate set of photos and a book so that the child can make a personal family album.

As you look through the completed album, spend time talking about the good things God has done. Read the Bible focus verse, and talk about this promise in light of the opportunities and struggles that you face.

For your prayer time, place some loose family photographs face down. Have each person choose one and then pray for the persons pictured.

Sharing Books

Bible Focus "All the believers were together and had everything in common" (Acts 2:44).

Materials books, bookplates, and index cards

Activity Talk about the blessing of being able to buy reading material. Read the Bible focus verse and encourage your child to have the desire to share books with others. Make some simple "library cards" from index cards for a few of your own books, and loan one or more books to a preschool friend.

Extra-special book ideas Record some favorite books on tape. Experiment with sound effects and different voices. Ring a chime at the end of every page so that your child can use the book tapes without adult supervision.

Pack a book for supper. Take books along to a restaurant. Have a family quiet time based on books while you're waiting to be served.

Sharing Magazines

Bible Focus   "We have come to share in Christ" (Heb. 3:14).

Materials   magazine subscriptions, your own and a friend's

Activity   Decide on two preschooler magazines that you would like to subscribe to for your child. Find a friend who also would like to subscribe to the magazines, and share the cost by subscribing to one in each child's name. When the magazines arrive, take turns reading them. For family quiet times, read all or part of a magazine, and talk about how a personal faith in Jesus applies to what you have read.

Go back to ideas that are especially interesting to your child, and build a quiet time around those ideas. From time to time, share a quiet time based on a magazine feature with the friend who shares your magazines. Do a suggested craft or activity, and then have a short time of discussion and prayer.

Preschooler magazines are available on the themes of health, nature, and Christian activities. (See References and Further Reading on page 142 for some specific titles.)

Extra-special idea for using magazines   Let your child cut a picture from a colorful seed or department store catalog. Paste the cutout onto a blank sheet of paper. Have your child tell a story about the picture, while you write down the words. Share the story as a way of telling about how Jesus is part of everyday living.

5

Not Just for Sundays

Devotions Using Sunday School Take-Home Papers

Families sometimes discover with great surprise that as simple a thing as this, a specific commitment of time for family worship, can have a transforming effect on everything that happens within the home.
—Larry Christenson, *The Christian Family*

Sunday school take-home papers hover precariously between treasure and trash. Since they often represent your preschooler's first experience with "school," your child's enthusiasm for Sunday school papers runs high. A young child wants you to look at every detail of every craft immediately, and the new artwork must be displayed in your home for at least twelve weeks! The parent, however, knows that there's a limit to how many pictures one refrigerator door can hold. Soon every suit-coat pocket, purse, and Bible seems to teem with forgotten papers from the nursery class, and since your child doesn't want to part with a one of them, you can't clean house until your little one is asleep.

The good news about Sunday school take-home papers is that they provide an excellent resource for parent-and-preschooler quiet times. Because take-home papers are prepared especially for your preschooler's age level, the illustrations, stories, and activities are well-suited to your child. Sunday school papers are new each week, so your child constantly has fresh material to share with you. At the same time, the materials you see usually have been used as part of the Sunday school lesson; when you read them to your child you reinforce the content of your church's Christian education program.

Even after those special moments of quiet time have passed, there can be a lot of life and learning left in your collection of take-home sheets. The following pages contain ideas for making the most of the materials your child brings home from church.

Activities from Sunday School Take-Home Papers

■ Special Suggestions for You. Many curriculum materials include regular suggestions for the preschooler's parent or family. Look for these special directions and choose to include at least one suggested activity or discussion in your quiet time routine. Take advantage of checklists and charts that might be included. These can keep you up-to-date on your child's learning activities.

■ Sunday School on Tuesday. Pick a special day each week to review your child's Sunday school lesson. Use the stories, activities, and prayers as the content of your quiet time together. Most papers include both a contemporary story and a simply told Bible story. Talk about a recent experience in your own home that fits the theme of the two stories you read.

■ Picture-Talk. Look carefully at the illustrations. Your child may show interest in some of the nonverbal ideas being told by the drawings. Talk about the child in the wheelchair who is attending Sunday school, the women who carried heavy water jugs to the well in Bible times, or other details that spark curiosity.

■ More of the Same.   If your child comes home excited about a fingerplay, a simple song, or a new prayer, look for ways to extend the activity. Write a new verse for the song or a second act to the fingerplay to reinforce your child's enthusiasm.

■ Sibling's Swap.   Encourage two or more children to play Sunday school. Take turns being the teacher, the song leader, the student. Encourage an older child to share a lesson from Sunday with a younger sibling or friend. Encourage an older child to be patient while a young sibling "teaches" a lesson, too.

■ Sunday Morning.   Try making Sunday morning a special time to prepare for worship. Have a simple breakfast together. Put some reminder of last week's Sunday school lesson on the table. Have a short review of last week's lesson while you eat. Pray for your teachers and pastor before you leave for church.

■ Invitation for a Friend.   Share a sample of your Sunday school material with a neighbor who doesn't attend church. Invite that person to visit your church. Pray before you make the visit and after you come home. Thank God that you and your child have the privilege of sharing Christ with others.

■ Signposts and Notes.   Use pages from your child's lessons on friendship, helpfulness, and sharing as reminders around the house. Display them at appropriate places—by the bathroom sink, above the washing machine, or in the tool shed, to remind family members of how God wants us to treat others. Thank your child for a pretty sign that helps you to remember to be kind, helpful, thankful, and joyful.

■ Personal Notes. Use one-sided coloring sheets as stationery for letters to relatives and friends. Let your child choose the picture to send. Include your child's handwritten "words" in the letter. Write "A picture for you from (your child's name)" on the letter and show your child how to mail it.

■ Learn How to Recycle Paper. Some nonprofit organizations collect recyclable paper as a fundraiser. Some businesses pay by the pound for recyclable paper. Let your child have some of the responsibilities for recycling in your home. Help your preschooler to understand that old paper can be made into new paper and that recycling paper can save trees. Make a "recycle box" as the last stop for Sunday school take-home papers.

Things to Make from Sunday School Take-Home Papers

■ Flannelgraph Boards. Glue flannel to the backs of some of your favorite illustrations from take-home papers. Then try sticking them to the back of a living room chair or sofa, or make a flannelgraph board by covering a piece of cardboard with flannel. For travel activities, glue a piece of flannel into the lid of a shoe box. Keep all your child's flannelgraph pieces inside the box. Use your flannelboards to review scripture verses or Sunday school materials.

■ Jigsaw Puzzles. Glue artwork to thin cardboard or poster board. Cut into jigsaw puzzles pieces. For a novel greeting card, make a puzzle from a page that contains a scripture verse on love or joy. Cut the pieces apart and put them into an envelope.

Deliver your card to someone who is sick or homebound. Share a devotional time with that person before you leave.

■ Missing and Matching.   Trace an illustration onto a plain sheet of paper. Glue the tracing onto a thin piece of posterboard or a file folder. Then glue the illustration to a stiff background. Cut the illustration into several logical parts. Let your child place the cutout pieces onto the tracing to reproduce the original picture.

Help your child with difficult puzzles, and talk about how God is the one who helps you when things get difficult for you. Reinforce the importance of patience, gratefulness, and trust as you work together on a hard skill.

■ My Own Activity Books.   Sort single-page takehomes into separate piles so that all coloring sheets, dot-to-dots, fingerplays, Bible stories, etc., are together. Though sorting is in itself an interesting learning activity for preschoolers, the real payoff comes from the fun activity books you can make from each pile. Stack like pages, punch along the left margin and bind with a piece of yarn. Use these activity books for rainy-day play, while traveling, or for family devotions. If your child's papers come in booklet form, bind these takehomes together in chronological order to make a longer storybook.

■ My Own Songbook.   Collect music sheets from take-home papers to make your own songbook. Older children might want to draw pictures to include in the book. Add an original song to the collection.

■ Memory Cards.   Take-home papers often have a Bible verse printed at the same spot each week. Collect these verses. Glue them onto cards. Keep them in a basket on your breakfast table. Every morning, pick a scripture verse to think about during the day. At night, talk about the thoughts you had. Encourage your child in the discipline of thinking about Jesus throughout the day. Or bind your cards together into a booklet of Scripture to memorize.

■ Lacing Cards.   Glue illustrations to stiff cardboard. Then punch holes around the perimeters of some of the main subjects in each picture. Buy colorful shoelaces or tape the tips of yarn pieces to use as sturdy laces. Make extra lacing cards for your child's Sunday school teacher or for a classmate.

■ Bookmarks to Baubles.   When your child wants to cut and paste, provide old take-home papers. Make bookmarks, gift tags, giftwrap, or Christmas tree decorations to share with family and friends. Encourage your child's willingness to tell the good news of Jesus to others.

Extra-Special Sunday School Ideas

■ Invite a Teacher to Lunch.   Invite your child's Sunday school teacher to your home. Have your child help with the preparations for a meal. Help your child make a simple gift to place at the teacher's plate. Have a short devotional time together. This is a good activity to help a preschooler overcome shyness in church and a good way of saying "thank you" to the adult who teaches your child.

■ My First Backpack.   Let your child take a backpack (book bag) to Sunday school so that Bible, offering money, and take-home papers can be kept together.

6

Special Ways to Pray

Devotions Based on Prayer

He prayeth best who loveth best
All things both great and small;
For the dear God who loveth us,
He made and loveth all.
—Coleridge

Somewhere along the way, our children learn how to answer the telephone, greet the mail carrier, and talk with the college student behind the grocery counter. Such simple communication skills are both taught and caught, since in addition to listening to parental instructions a child learns through imitation. Prayer is another kind of conversation. Short memorized prayers, lessons about God, and stories of believers who pray probably can increase a preschooler's interest in prayer. Nothing outside of actual prayer itself, however, will do more toward encouraging a child to pray.

Prayer is the core of our relational faith. Because of Christ's sacrifice on the cross, we always are welcomed into the Father's arms. Our children have the opportunity to see this truth when we regularly turn to God. Honesty, simplicity, and sincerity should be evident in our prayers. From early on, children should know the privilege of pouring out their joys and sorrows before the throne of grace.

We shouldn't be red-faced when a five-year-old prays for Jesus to help him make his rocket. God understands (even more than we do) what weighs on our children's minds. Nor should we fear our four-year-old's bold requests for God to find her puppy or heal her grandma. God is able to communicate consistent care in such situations. In fact, while we fumble with earth-bound explanations on the way God hears and responds, our child's unassuming faith might soar beyond ours to a clearer view of the nature of God.

In celebration of our friendship with God, let us joyfully lead our children into God's presence. The following pages contain ideas on special ways to pray.

How We Pray

Bible Focus   "Hear my prayer, O LORD" (Ps. 86:6).

Use the following activities as lead-ins for short times of prayer. Add to the following Bible focus verses on prayer as you find them in the course of your own study. Encourage your child to suggest ways and times to pray.

We Pray Privately

Bible Focus   "When you pray, go into your room, close the door and pray to [God] who is unseen" (Matt. 6:6).

Activity   Read the Bible focus verse. Say: "Other people don't have to hear what we say when we talk to God. We can be all by ourselves when we pray." Remind your child that God really listens to prayers. Try some times of silent prayer, at grace or before naptime, so that your child will gain confidence in praying on his or her own.

We Pray as Jesus Taught Us

Bible Focus   "This is how you should pray: 'Our Father in heaven, hallowed be your name, your kingdom come, your will be done on earth as it is in heaven. Give us this day our daily bread. Forgive us our debts, as we also have forgiven our debtors. And lead us not into temptation, but deliver us from the evil one.' " (Matt. 6:9-13).

Activity   Talk about the Lord's Prayer. Say the familiar version that is used in your church. Then talk about one line in the Lord's Prayer. Pray that short portion of the prayer with your child. Over a period of days or weeks, repeat this activity until you've talked about each line of the prayer.

We Pray with Thankful Hearts

Bible Focus   "Be joyful always; pray continually; give thanks in all circumstances, for this is God's will for you in Christ Jesus" (1 Thess. 5:16-18).

Activity   Read and talk about the Bible focus verse. Make it a habit to include praise and thanksgiving in every prayer. Share some simple praise songs with your child. Close your eyes and sing a song of praise to God. Point out that a song can be a prayer.

We Pray with a Hearty Amen!

Bible Focus   "Amen. Come, Lord Jesus. The grace of the Lord Jesus be with God's people. Amen" (Rev. 22:20-21).

Activity   Read the Bible's final prayer and benediction to your child. Ask: "What do the 'amens' mean?" Tell your child that you can say "Yes, let it be so!" instead of "amen" because this is what the word *amen* means. Read the verses again, substituting "Yes, let it be so!" for "amen." Then pray your own prayer and end with "Yes, let it be so!" Show how using the "amen" ending can help us think about praying for what God wants.

Pray for Each Other

Bible Focus "Therefore confess your sins to each other and pray for each other so that you may be healed. The prayer of a righteous man is powerful and effective" (James 5:16).

Activity The following hands-on projects can stimulate your child's interest in prayer:

■ A Prayer Box. Unroll a four- to six-foot length of bathroom tissue and place it on a hard surface. On each perforated square, write a short reminder of a family prayer request with a felt-tipped marker. Include the names of your friends and other people. Carefully reroll the tissue strip. Open the side of an empty boutique-style facial tissue box and place the tissue roll inside. Feed the first square of the tissue roll through the slot in the top. Then tape the side of the box closed. Write "Our Prayer Box" on the front panel. Daily have each family member pull off a tissue square. Form a prayer circle and have each person say a short prayer for the person or need on his or her tissue sheet.

■ The Picture-Prayer Journal. Fill an inexpensive snapshot album with pictures of family, friends, and things of special interest. Include cutouts from magazines, church mailings, etc., to cover different situations for which you wish to pray. Then sit with your child and say a short sentence prayer to go with each picture.

■ Prayer Napkins. Write the name of each dinner guest on a paper napkin. Let your child fold the napkins and put one at each spot. As part of your prayer before the meal, go around the table and let each person say a sentence prayer for the person whose name is written on his or her napkin.

■ Praying Hands, Praying Hearts. Cut out praying hands and hide them throughout the house. Whenever one is found, take a moment to pray a prayer of thanks or intercession for someone in your family.

■ Telephone Prayer Chain. If your church has a prayer chain that relays prayer requests over the telephone, include your child when possible. When you are asked to pray, ask your child to pray also. Stop your work immediately and pray a simple prayer that does not jeopardize the confidentiality of the request. Thank your child for being a partner in prayer.

Extra-special ideas on prayer

■ What Shall We Pray? Read the James 5:16 Bible focus verse again. Talk about some of its principles: God wants us to be truthful about our problems and needs. God wants us to share our troubles and joys with other Christians. We should pray for one another. And when we do, we can start by asking God to forgive our own failures and mistakes. God hears our prayers and can heal us, physically and in other ways too. It is good and right that we ask for God's help.

■ See how Daniel prayed in Dan. 6:10, and copy his prayer pattern for a day. Kneel in the morning, at noon, and at night and give the Lord prayers of thanks.

■ See how Jesus prayed in Luke 6:12. Talk about Jesus' prayer life, then pray in a quiet outdoor setting.

■ Memorize 1 Thess. 5:17 and take it to heart. Throughout the day ask each other, "When was the last time you prayed?" Share your most recent prayer or confess that your mind has not been on God. Then say a short prayer with your child.

7

Outdoors with God

Devotions on God's World

[Look] through nature up to nature's God.
—Alexander Pope

To a young child the outdoors can be both athletic arena and art gallery. A preschooler can run and jump and play with reckless exhilaration and a moment later silently ponder the intricate design of a firefly in the grass. Both experiences are tied to the God who created all things.

You can have devotions outdoors whether you know a little or a lot about nature. A backyard or nearby vacant lot is all the wilderness a young child needs for exploration. You can learn about nature as your child learns. Library books and programs put on by your local Audubon Society chapter or nearby parks can encourage you in your efforts to share the wonders of creation with your child.

Though the quiet times that follow in this chapter are designated for two- to five-year-olds, even younger children relish outdoor excursions. Begin in your child's infancy to share the wonderful assortment of outdoor colors, textures, and smells. Continue to expand your explorations as your child grows.

Days for Discovery

Bible Focus   "This is the day the LORD has made" (Ps. 118:24).

Materials   magnifying glass

Activity   Read the Bible focus verse and then set out on a nature walk. Walk slowly, letting your child lead. Get down on hands and knees to look closely at the small things your child finds.

Examine things with a magnifying glass. Talk about the things that hold your child's attention. At the middle and end of your walk, repeat the Bible focus verse together.

Extra-special walk ideas

■ A Rain Walk.   Use "[God] . . . sends rain" (Matt. 5:45) as your Bible focus verse. Put on raincoats and boots and take a playful walk in warm gentle rain. As you walk, talk about God and the blessing of rain.

■ A Dawn Walk.   Use "Morning by morning, O Lord, you hear my voice" (Ps. 5:3) as your Bible focus verse. Take a walk in the early morning. Sing a song and pray along your way.

■ A Night Walk.   Use "You, [Lord], bring darkness, it becomes night, and all the beasts of the forest prowl" (Ps. 104:20) as your Bible focus verse. Before going to bed, take a walk to see what animals "prowl" in your area. Talk about how each animal has a part in God's plan. Thank Jesus for the night.

■ A Touch Walk.   Use "When I consider . . . the works of your fingers" (Ps. 8:3) as your Bible focus verse.

Find objects that are smooth, cool, rough, fuzzy, etc. Emphasize that God made everything from stars to flowers.

■ An Eye Walk.   Use "God saw all that he had made, and it was very good" (Gen. 1:31) as your Bible focus verse. Sit quietly in one spot and let your eyes do the "walking." What is the smallest thing you see? The biggest? How many green things can you find? When you are done with your "walk," close your eyes and listen for things that God has made.

Exercise

Bible Focus   "You [God] created my inmost being" (Ps. 139:13).

Materials   outdoor space for exercises

Activity   Read the Bible focus verse. Talk about the joys of running, jumping, and playing outside. Explain that even our happy play can be done as a kind of praise to God. Do some jogging or directed exercises while talking about how different parts of our bodies work. Then rest and tell your child that you enjoyed sharing this exercise experience. Talk about how we should take good care of our bodies so that we can serve God with as much strength and energy as possible. Pray a short prayer of thanks for hands, feet, lungs, etc. Help your child to think of short thanksgiving sentences to say.

Treasures

Bible Focus   "Give thanks to the LORD" (Ps. 105:1).

Materials   a collection of nature finds and a place to display them

Activity   Together collect some nature objects that fascinate your child. Pick up things that nature has discarded, not flowers, nests, animals, and other things that need to be outside. Encourage your child to arrange the finds in one of the following ways:

Spread things out on a tray so that everything is easy to see.

Collect 12 interesting things, one for each compartment in an egg carton.

Glue little treasures onto a piece of driftwood

Glue natural decorations onto the lid of a shoebox in which to keep additional treasures

Then have your child share the collection with an interested person. Talk about each natural object and close with a prayer of thanks to God for the interesting things you have seen.

In Every Season

Bible Focus   "As long as the earth endures, seedtime and harvest, cold and heat, summer and winter, day and night will never cease" (Gen. 8:22).

Materials   calendar, notebook, and a special outside place

Activity   Use the calendar to talk about the months and seasons of the year: What month is it? What season is it? Read the Bible focus verse and talk about seasons as part of God's plan.

Pick a special outdoor place to explore. What are some special things about it in this season? Write down the things your child observes and explain that you will save these notes until the next visit. Return to your special place in every season. Continue to take notes. Then read your observations from all the months and talk about God's promise as revealed in the Bible focus verse. Thank God for the beauty and blessing of each season.

Meet the Animals

Bible Focus   "God made the wild animals according to their kinds" (Gen. 1:25).

Materials   pictures of animals or real animals, Bible

Activity   Read the Bible focus verse and then look at the variety of animals God has made by going to the zoo, reading a nature magazine or book, or taking a walk.

Point out that people in the Bible were fascinated by animals, just as we are. Read some of the following Bible passages and let your child raise a hand whenever an animal is named. As you read other scripture verses, keep in mind the animals God created.

1 Kings 10:22:   "The king had a fleet of trading ships. . . . Once every three years it returned carrying gold, silver and ivory, and *apes* and *baboons.*"

Prov. 6:5-6:   "Free yourself, like a *gazelle* from the hand of the hunter, like a *bird* from the snare of the fowler. Go to the *ant,* you sluggard; consider its ways and be wise."

Matt. 6:19:   "Do not store up for yourselves treasures on earth, where *moth* and rust destroy."

Matt. 19:24:   "Again I tell you, it is easier for a *camel* to go through the eye of a needle than for a rich man to enter the kingdom of God."

Luke 9:58:   "*Foxes* have holes and *birds* of the air have nests, but the Son of Man has no place to lay his head."

Thank God for the animals you have seen and talked about during your quiet time.

Where Jesus Walked

Bible Focus   "Jesus, tired as he was from the journey, sat down by the well" (John 4:6).

Materials   one or more outdoor settings, Bible

Activity   Read the Bible focus verse. Point out that Jesus spent many, many hours walking from town to town. He got tired and he got thirsty just as we do on long walks. Say that Jesus also had time to look at the sky, the trees, the birds, and the land just as we do when we walk. Then go on a walk and think about Jesus.

When the wind brushes your cheek, talk about times when Jesus felt the wind (while in a boat calming the storm, etc.).

When you walk along the shore and put your feet in the sand, talk about Jesus who spent time with men in fishing boats along the Sea of Galilee.

When you enjoy the shade of trees, talk about times when Jesus prayed among the olive trees.

When you feel the heat of the desert, talk about Jesus' days in the wilderness.

As you read the Bible, look for additional passages that give you clues to the sights, sounds, feels, smells, and tastes of the environment Jesus knew. With your child, let similar environmental conditions remind you that Jesus truly walked on this earth. Thank Jesus that he came to earth to show us what God is like.

Buckets

Bible Focus   "Holy, holy, holy is the Lord Almighty; the whole earth is full of his glory" (Isa. 6:3).

Materials   shovels, buckets, and sand, or containers and water

Activity   Play with your child in sand or in water. Fill and dump containers. Experiment with how much water or sand different containers can hold. Talk about the words *empty* and *full*. Show their meanings by emptying and filling containers. Then have fun learning that empty containers are filled with invisible air.

After you have put the toys away, tell the story of how Isaiah had a wonderful look at what God was like (Isa. 6:1-8). Tell it in your own words. Make it an exciting, awesome listening experience for your child. Then repeat the seraphs' words in the Bible focus verse. Talk about how the earth is filled with God's glory. Explain that this means God's glory is everywhere. Try to imagine being able to see God's glory as Isaiah did.

Then talk about the empty and full buckets you played with. Talk about when you could see a bucket filled and when you could not see a bucket filled (because it held invisible air). Even though we can't see "glory" as we see sand or water, God can fill our hearts with it. God can also fill our lives with love, peace, patience, and joy. Ask: "What would you like God to fill your life with?" Tell your own desires. Pray: *Heavenly Father, fill us with your* (name one trait). *Thank you. Amen.*

Take Good Care of God's Earth

Bible Focus "The LORD God took the man and put him in the Garden of Eden to work it and take care of it" (Gen. 2:15).

Materials large bag for collecting litter

Activity Read the Bible focus verse and share ideas about what Eden might have been like. Point out that it was God's plan for humans to take care of the natural world. Talk about how humans treat the natural world today. As a way of saying to others that you love God and God's creation, spend a quiet time picking up litter. At the end of your work, affirm your child's good deed.

Then pray: *Dear God, we love you and the world you made. We are sorry when we and others treat nature unkindly. Thank you for the time and strength we had today to pick up litter. We did it, Lord, to show our love for you and the world you made. Amen.*

Around a Campfire

Bible Focus   "I will tell of all your wonders" (Ps. 9:1).

Materials   a campfire

Activity   Build a "Story Fire." Let your child collect tinder, kindling, and fuel for this campfire, but don't let the child work around the burning wood. Teach simple safety practices to go along with building, burning, and enjoying a campfire.

When the night is dark and the fire is blazing, gather within the golden light. Explain that this is a "Story Fire" because, just as you are doing tonight, people for thousands of years have grouped around nighttime fires to hear stories. Think about the Israelites wandering in the desert, the Wise Men traveling to find baby Jesus, the shepherds who watched flocks in the night, and Paul on his missionary journeys. No doubt all these people gathered around fires to talk at night. Tell your favorite Bible story or pick one related to fire: the burning bush (Exodus 3), Elijah on Mount Carmel (1 Kings 18), the men in the furnace (Daniel 3) and Paul's shipwreck on Malta (Acts 27 and 28). (Reading a book about storytelling and listening to good storytellers can improve your own skills.)

Close your evening around the fire with some singing and a prayer.

Appendix

Personalizing Devotions for Your Family

As you conduct your private devotions and read and listen to proclamations of the Good News, look for ways to create new devotional times with your preschooler. This section concludes with a listing of learning experiences for active preschoolers and a references and further reading list. These lists, however, only serve to give you a brief idea of the many, many appropriate activities and resources available for your quiet times with active preschoolers.

The following form can be used to record your own ideas for quiet times with your preschooler. Look for ways to personalize your devotional times, keeping in mind the joys and concerns that face your family and others around you. May God continue to bless the special moments you share with your child and with God.

Quiet Time Idea for _____, **age** ____:

Source of Idea:

Appropriate Bible Focus Verse:

Materials Needed:

Outline of Activity:

Learning Experiences for Active Preschoolers*

Active Learning

1. Exploring with the use of all five senses—hearing, smelling, touching, seeing, tasting.
2. Choosing materials and subjects of interest to explore by direct contact and experience.
3. Having hands-on contact with materials that can be manipulated, combined, and/or transformed.
4. Developing skills with tools and equipment.
5. Using large muscles for ball playing, swinging, running, etc.
6. Taking care of personal needs such as brushing teeth.

Using Language

7. Talking about things of personal interest.
8. Describing objects, events, and relationships.
9. Putting feelings into words.
10. Having own words written down and read back.
11. Having language fun: poems, fingerplays, listening to and making up stories and songs.

Representing Experiences and Ideas

12. Recognizing familiar objects by sound, touch, taste, and smell.

*This list is adapted from approximately 50 "key experiences" compiled by the High/Scope Educational Research Foundation to serve as guideposts for planning and evaluating developmentally valid programs for young children. The original list appears in *Young Children in Action: A Manual for Preschool Educators*, Mary Hohmann, Bernard Banet, and David P. Weikart (Ypsilanti, Michigan: High/Scope Press, 1981), pp. 3-6.

13. Relating pictures and models to real places and things.
14. Pretending, imitating, and acting out animals and characters.
15. Making models from clay or blocks.
16. Drawing and painting.

Developing Logical Reasoning

17. Investigating and describing characteristics; for example, Jonah's face is sad.
18. Noticing and describing similarities and differences; for example, the sailors' faces are sad, too, but the big fish looks happy.
19. Noticing and expressing differences caused by characteristics that are not present: This tree is not brown.
20. Thinking about more than one characteristic at a time: James has a fishing boat that is big and brown.
21. Distinguishing between some and all.
22. Using comparisons—bigger, smaller, darker, louder, etc.
23. Arranging things by length or size.
24. Comparing amounts: more, less, same.
25. Using one-to-one correspondence: Make a Valentine for each aunt—four aunts, four cards.
26. Counting, while pointing to objects and by rote.

Understanding Time and Space

27. Fitting things together and taking things apart.
28. Rearranging objects to take on different sizes and shapes: The stack of magazines makes a tower. Spread out, the magazines make a highway.

29. Observing things and places from a number of vantage points.
30. Experiencing and talking about the position of things and people: I am next to Daddy. I am on his tummy.
31. Experiencing and talking about the movement of things and people.
32. Experiencing and talking about distances between things and people.
33. Experiencing the design and movement of one's own body.
34. Learning the location of things in the home, church, and neighborhood: Toby, will you help by getting a pencil for me?
35. Learning to understand how space is represented in drawings and pictures.
36. Recognizing and describing shapes.
37. Planning and completing what one has planned: I'm going to build a train track right through the kitchen.
38. Telling what happened in the past.
39. Anticipating future events and getting ready.
40. Starting and stopping an action according to directions.
41. Noticing, describing, and representing the order of events.
42. Experiencing and describing rates of movement.
43. Using time units such as this morning, yesterday, tomorrow.
44. Comparing times: A long time ago, when it was new, etc.
45. Recognizing that clocks and calendars are used to mark the passage of time.
46. Observing the seasonal changes in nature.

References and Further Reading

Chapter 1   Preparing Your Own Heart: Devotions for Parents

Campbell, Ross. *How to Really Love Your Child*. Wheaton: Victor Books, 1987.

Christenson, Larry. *The Christian Family*. Minneapolis: Bethany, 1970. (Out of print.)

Drescher, John M. *If I Were Starting My Family Again*. Nashville: Abingdon, 1979.

Klug, Ron and Lyn. *Bible Readings for Parents*. Minneapolis: Augsburg, 1982.

Schaeffer, Edith. *What Is a Family?*. Old Tappen, N.J.: Revell, 1982.

Swindoll, Charles R. *You and Your Child*. Nashville: Thomas Nelson, 1982.

Tengbom, Mildred and Luverne. *Bible Readings for Families*. Minneapolis: Augsburg, 1980.

Chapter 2   Every Day with God: Devotions for Children

Baehr, Theodore, et al. *The Movie-Video Guide for Christian Families: Selecting the Best in Home Video and TV Movies for Your Family*. Nashville: Thomas Nelson, 1987.

Baratta-Lorton, Mary. *Workjobs: Activity-Centered Learning for Early Childhood*. Reading, Mass.: Addison-Wesley, 1972. (Out of print.)

Coleman, William L. *Making TV Work for Your Family*. Minneapolis: Bethany, 1983.

Hansen, Harlan. *Parenting the 4- to 6-Year-Old*. (Growing with God's Child series). Minneapolis: Augsburg, 1986.

Hohmann, Mary; Banet, Bernard; and Weikart, David P. *Young Children in Action: A Manual for Preschool Educators*. Ypsilanti, Mich.: High/Scope Press, 1978.

McDaniel, Elsiebeth. *You and Your Preschoolers*. (Effective Teaching Series). Chicago: Moody, 1975. (Out of print.)

Mow, Anna A. *Preparing Your Child to Love God*. Grand Rapids: Zondervan, 1983. (Out of print.)

Murphy, Elspeth Campbell. David and I Talk to God series. Hardcover Psalm Books for Children series. Elgin, Ill.: David C. Cook, 1981–87. (Two series with several titles in each.)

Richards, Larry. *International Children's Bible Handbook*. Ft. Worth: Sweet, 1986.

Rodning, Carol J. *Parenting the 0- to 3-Year-Old* (Growing with God's Child series). Minneapolis: Augsburg, 1988.

"Talking with Children about Death." (A free booklet available from Public Inquiries, National Institute of Mental Health, 5600 Fishers Lane, Rockville MD 20857.)

Chapter 3   Special Days with God: Devotions for Holidays

Dobson, Shirley and Gaither, Gloria. *Let's Make a Memory*. Waco: Word, 1986.

Erickson, Donna. *Prime Time Together . . . with Kids*. Minneapolis: Augsburg, 1989.

Chapter 4   Storytime with God: Devotions Using Books for Children

Batchelor, Mary. *The Children's Bible in 365 Stories*. Batavia, Ill: Lion, 1985. (Out of print.)

Beers, V. Gilbert. *My Picture Bible to See and to Share*. Wheaton: Victor Books, 1982.

Beers, V. Gilbert and Beers, Ronald A. *Growing God's Way to See and Share*. Wheaton: Victor Books, 1987.

Clubhouse, Jr. Panoma, Calif.: Focus on the Family. (Magazine for preschoolers with a Christian emphasis.)

Ettner, Dann J. *The Seven Days of Creation*. St. Louis: Concordia, 1986. (This book contains songs and finger puppets.) (Out of print.)

Frank, Penny. *Gideon Fights for God* and *Solomon's Golden Temple* (The Lion Story Bible Series). Batavia, Ill.: Lion, 1987. (This series includes a number of short Bible stories from the Old and New Testaments.)

Graves, Ruth. *The RIF Guide to Encouraging Young Readers*. Garden City, N.Y.: Doubleday, 1987.

Hockermann, Dennis. My Bible Book Series. Elgin, Ill.: David C. Cook, 1987.

Lashbrook, Marilyn. *Get Lost Little Brother* (The Me Too! Book Series). Dallas: Roper Press, 1988. (Series includes other titles.)

Lindvall, Ella K. *The Bible Illustrated for Little Children*. Chicago: Moody, 1985.

Muir, Virginia. *The One-Year Bible Story Book*. Wheaton: Tyndale, 1988.

O'Neal, Debbie Trafton. *My Read-and-Do Bible Storybook*. Minneapolis: Augsburg, 1989.

Taylor, Kenneth N. *The Bible in Pictures for Little Eyes*. Chicago: Moody, 1956.

Tudor, Tasha. *First Poems of Childhood*. New York: Putnam, 1978.

Turtle Magazine for Preschool Kids. Indianapolis: Children's Better Health Institute. (Magazine with a health and safety emphasis.)

Your Big Backyard. Washington, D.C.: National Wildlife Federation. (Magazine for preschoolers with a nature emphasis.)

Chapter 5 Not Just for Sundays: Devotions Using Sunday School Take-Home Papers

Check with your local Christian bookstore or denominational publishing house for information on current materials, in addition to those being used in your child's Sunday school class.

Chapter 6 Special Ways to Pray: Devotions Based on Prayer

Alexander, Martha. *Poems and Prayers for the Very Young.* New York: Random House, 1973.

McKissack, Patricia and Fredrick. *When Do You Talk to God?.* Minneapolis: Augsburg, 1986.

Schreivogel, Paul A. *More Prayers for Small Children.* Minneapolis: Augsburg, 1988.

Schreivogel, Paul A. *Small Prayers for Small Children.* Minneapolis: Augsburg, 1980.

Tangvald, Christine Harder. *A Child's Book of Prayers.* Elgin, Ill.: David C. Cook, 1987.

Tengbom, Mildred. *Mealtime Prayers.* Minneapolis: Augsburg, 1985.

Chapter 7 Outdoors with God: Devotions on God's World

Barrett, Ethel. *Storytelling, It's Easy.* Grand Rapids: Zondervan, 1987.

Williamson, Denise J. *Bible Readings on God's Creation.* Minneapolis: Augsburg, 1987.